Rhymes to the Rescue

to the Rescue

by **Don Aslett**

200 USEFUL VERSES

Dedicated to
the author who
penned our
first nursery
rhyme.

President &
Sister Southworth
May you find value
in verse!
Don Aslett
2020

Published by
Marsh Creek Press
711 South 2nd Avenue
Pocatello ID 83201
DonAslettAuthor@gmail.com

Books are available for business
Or quantity discounts
208-236-6906

ISBN: 978-1-7341396-0-0 (hardcover)
ISBN: 978-1-7341396-1-7 (softcover)

Manufactured in USA

Some of don's favorite poem excerpts

THE SPELL OF THE YUKON

I wanted the gold, and I sought it;
I scrabbled and mucked like a slave.
Was it famine or scurvy—I fought it;
I hurled my youth into a grave.
I wanted the gold, and I got it—
Came out with a fortune last fall,—
Yet somehow life's not what I thought it,
And somehow the gold isn't all.

—*Robert Service*

PREPAREDNESS

For all your days prepare,
And meet them ever alike:
When you are the anvil, bear—
When you are the hammer, strike.

—*Edwin Markham*

All seems infected that the infected Spy;
As all looks yellow to the Jaundiced Eye.

—*Alexander Pope*

THE HAMMERS

Noise of hammers once I heard
Many hammers, busy hammers,
Beating, shaping night and day.
Shaping, beating dust and clay
To a palace, saw it reared:
Saw the hammers laid away.

And I listened, and I heard
Hammers beating, night and day
In the palace newly reared,
Beating it into dust and clay:
Other hammers, muffled hammers,
Silent hammers of decay.

—*Ralph Hodgson*

DEGREE OF VALUES

My daughter has her Master's
My son his Ph.D.
But father is the only one around this house
Who has a J.O.B.

—*A. Thomas*

MAN-MAKING

We are all blind until we see,
That in the human plan
Nothing is worth the making,
If it does not make the man.
Why builds these cities glorious
If man unbuilded goes?
In vain we build the work
Unless the builder also grows

— *Edwin Markham*

TO ALTHEA, FROM PRISON

Stone walls do not a prison make,
Nor iron bars a cage:
Minds innocent and quiet take
That for an hermitage;
If I have freedom in my love,
And my soul is free,
Angels alone, that soar above,
Enjoy such liberty

—*Richard Lovelace*

My soul, sit thou a patent looker-on;
Judge not the play before the play is done:
Her plot hath many changes;
Every day speaks a new scene;
The last act crowns the play

—*Francis Quarles*

THE WATER MILL

Learn to make the most of life,
Lose no happy day.
Time will ne'er return again—
Sweet chance thrown away.
Leave no tender word unsaid,
But love while life shall last:
The mill will never grind,
With the water that has passed.

— *Sarah Doudney*

Poetry with a Promise

Welcome to a new, unique adventure in reading! You will quickly recognize your own thinking and opinions in this rhyming verse, discovering strong messages that are ready to use.

Don Aslett

TABLE OF CONTENTS

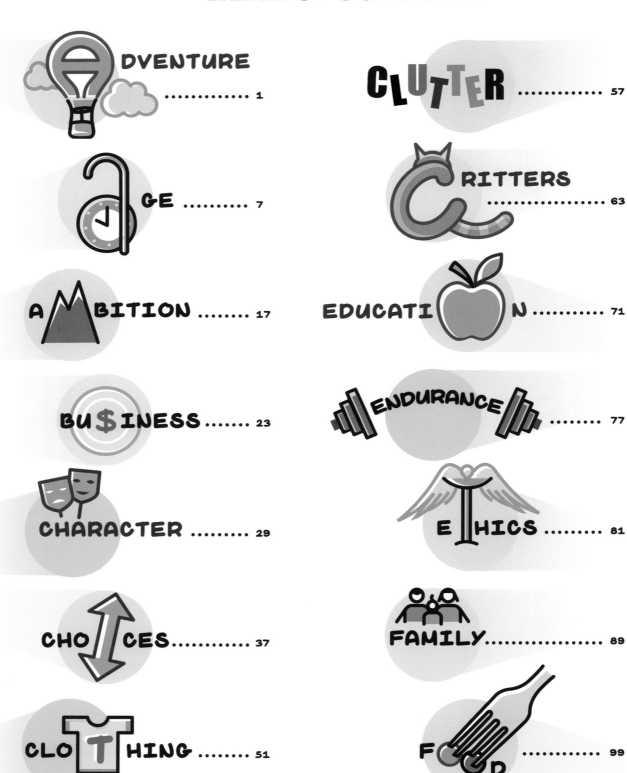

Rhymes to the Rescue

ADVENTURE

Stretching

Prim and proper has its place,
As does any social grace,
But sometimes a fresh idea or two
Can unwrinkle a stoic face.

De-cage yourself for a season,
Not surrendering morality
Just let out some pent-up emotion—NOW!
Done with integrity.

Fall in love again,
More seasoned than before
Find intimacy in holding hands
Letting charity keep the score.

Don't get wild! But abandon mild,
And venture toward bold
Liberate your style somehow
The "routine" is getting old.

Stick out your neck, by heck,
Jump in and learn to swim!
Giant trees that savor breeze
Have many a stretched-out limb.

Don Aslett

A Drifter's Dream

I see a vagrant, scruffy and worn,
Walking my homeward road,
I slow enough to view the man
And appraise the weight of his load.

Be it curiosity, maybe envy,
But something stirred my soul,
An urge to trade him places,
A recurring, passing goal.

He ignited a wanderlust
Latent in my soul,
To be free from all clocks' demand,
With only pack and bedroll.

A trigger for the wanderer
I think is in all mankind,
Something out in front of safe,
Something out there to find.

Found myself considering
Trudging from door to door,
Becoming a vagabond or pilgrim
Wouldn't mean that I'd be poor!

Trade my briefcase for his backpack
Sure it crossed my mind,
In his asphalt-dominated calendar
More freedom I would find,

Accepting any destination
That carefree fortune gives
Unlike all the scheduled ventures
Within the world I live.

I didn't see a derelict
But sensed royalty austere,
An adventurer? Explorer?
Pilgrim? Or maybe pioneer?

Homeless by choice, I gather,
Maybe a black sheep of the rich,
Perhaps discouraged or choosing freedom,
Does it matter which?

I doubted that most of the cars
That kept on whizzing by
Had any more important needs
Or better dreams than this guy.

Perhaps I'll never understand
This sudden brain attack
To stay and meet my hobo friend,
And trade my briefcase for his pack!

Dodged Bullets

Dodged a bullet? Made your day?
Be careful of the ricochet.

This time call it a lucky spin,
But bullets seldom miss again.

Ducked an outcome you deserved?
A pending lawsuit never served?

Perhaps an overlooked scratch or scrape
Followed by a clear path of escape.

Of shady deeds short of good sense,
Memory leaves lasting fingerprints.

Any secrets well tucked away
Are poised for a resurfacing day.

Even when repentance bound
Some consequences will stick around.

Be it words or the slightest thievery
Your conscience will give you misery.

As the risks from "bullets" never change
Best advice...STAY OUT OF RANGE.

Don Aslett

Soil Satisfaction

Far greater than cities and suburbs sterile
Are the simple joys of being raised rural.
Those memories with others I can share
As a big part of me still lives there.

How blessed the life when lived outdoors,
Braving frost to do the chores
Such freedoms! Who could ask for more
Than living rich when times were poor?

Blisters and suntan were badges earned
Worth was measured by daylight burned
Sting of winter to summer sweat
Everywhere the ethic—earn what you get.

"You better beat the sun out of bed!"
And "You can eat after stock is fed."
Had a headstart toward an MBA
Got all the basics in FFA

Posts and rows gave pride when straight,
Ever scheming to invent a perfect gate
Finding balance on a one-leg, milking stool,
Grinding sparks when sharpening a tool,

Learning to drive when nine or ten,
Duty to root out the skunks' new den;
Ringing clank of the granary door
Like writing my own musical score,

Aroma of hay during its 3-day cure
And ever the fragrance of fresh manure,
Accepting the elements though want to cuss,
That taste and cough from the harrow's dust,

With sun-chapped lips, one still could smile,
Hats and boots were necessity, not style,
Gloves wore out—were seldom lost,
Homegrown, homemade, lower cost.

Sound and smell have awesome reach
And nature will never cease to teach...
No matter our status in this earthly race
Soil is our final resting place.

ADVENTURE

5

Pioneer Spirit?

So rare this role of a pioneer
Who daily dodges failure's spear,
There are few now who venture forth
To deepest south and farthest north.

Wide awake, eve of despair,
Still forging on in the worst of fear,
A secure life is long passed away,
It's the firing line every single day.

Different, yes, from all their peers,
No park or reverse in all their gears.
Builders in sincere pursuit
Plant trees, but never taste their fruit.

Discomfort? They've had their turn
Watched plans, hopes, and bridges burn,
Some blood and skin left in the field,
Untimely death, but quest fulfilled.

We sing and praise these pioneers
Even bow our heads and shed some tears,
But soon forgotten who blazed the trail,
Who cleared the path, and set the sail.

Real pioneers seldom sit in camp
They're off to build with pick and lamp.
The critics cower in their wake
Safe harbor observers' role they take.

Why in safety net do we choose to stay?
It's our turn in this modern day!
Are we content as squatters on social fix?
Is pathfinding left to politics?

Horizon's unconquered, unexplored,
Fat and happy, entertained and bored,
Willing to join any trail that's made,
Slow to emerge from safety's shade.

Guarded wealth, financial fears,
Over-funded are not pioneers!
So where are the venturers of today?
Do we all let GPS map our way?

With wars and world turmoil mess
Who's spearheading today's wilderness?
Peacemakers and pilgrims are overdue,
Tribulation a plenty. Where are you?

Don Aslett

Dying with a Shiny Shovel

Where I grew up it was cool
To have your own shovel, a useful tool

A true honor on the ranch—
A shiny shovel, never came by chance

For what's well-used will show some wear
And have a polished, productive glare.

A goal exclaimed often when I spoke
Was to own a shiny shovel when I croak

I vowed to keep it mud-free and sharp
Up to the day I'd play the harp.

But hark! My life cannot yet stop—
My shovel now sits rusting in the shop!

How life follows the tale of that tool
Where luster is lost to Nature's rule.

Don Aslett

Creaking

A few years ago I seemed a bit quicker
Flowers smelled sweeter, and hair a bit thicker.
The ground is now so much farther away
Then when I played ball in my sports heyday.

Climbing stairs took less effort and rigor,
Print on a page was clearer and bigger,
The padding has left my bottom and knees,
Must hire young guys to trim my trees.

My grip is weaker, my stamina less,
There are fewer people I care to impress.
Irritations have profoundly increased,
The need to play or travel has almost ceased.

Who cares if my socks don't match my shoes?
There is more to give and less to lose.
Marathons have turned into a stroll,
My bed calls out...and rest is my goal.

It happened quite gradually I must admit—
Now too old to sprint but too young to quit.
Something has surely gone out of whack,
But if granted the wish—**I'd never go back!**

The Upside of Old

Sure, we all expect some aging
Life's sequence we must accept,
Some dimming of eyes and changing in size,
The occasional attack of inept.

But "old" is a grimmer story
It seems to emerge overnight,
It's a whopping surprise, when you realize
You've lost that "youthful" flight.

Decline over time creeps up slowly
With wrinkles and a pain or two,
An occasional fall, and writing's a scrawl,
Find it hard to recall people you knew.

Then comes that fatal morning
You wake up and have to admit
You've turned the page, become an old sage,
"Sir" or "Ma'am," a perfect fit.

Drivers have to dodge you,
Others keep track of your pills.
Travel by scooter, you're a slower commuter
You need help up the smallest of hills.

Competition has vanished forever
All trivia irritates,
You can now be a clown or talk of the town
As seconds mount up on your plate.

People give you more room, stay out of your way
Everyone demands that you sit,
They covet what you own, keep what you loan,
Figuring you'll surely forget.

Family suggests the new senior center
Room and board for retirees.
Age is no joke, docs predict when you'll croak,
Advise surgery for hips and for knees.

Remedies for comfort or pain
And benefits for seniors abound;
People hold doors, clean up your floors,
There's programs to take you around.

Rest when you want, no questions asked,
Surf channels on a big screen TV,
Not to mention, you're now center of attention
Being so close to eternity.

The brighter side of these numbered years,
Statistics are now on your side.
Thank your lucky star, you made it this far,
There's more miles in this old hide!

Don Aslett

Packaging Pains

It could be me, I'll bet you too,
Are lids now harder to unscrew?

Every package I try to strip,
Good heavens! Seems I've lost my grip;
In unwrapping I don't get far,
Even have trouble with a candy bar.

The purchase there before my eyes
 In plastic clamshell is my prize,
And oh how happy I shall be
 If I can get this dang thing free!

Can't find an edge to start or peel,
switchblade needed to break the seal,
That scored tear-mark seldom works,
Immune to all my pulls and jerks.

My fingernails just can't compete,
As I stretch, rip, tug, and beat.
Angry struggles don't make a dent,
Must fetch a sharper instrument.

So well named, "blister" pack,·
The Band-Aid box next needs a whack.
Last resort, I'll use my teeth,
That plywood cardboard could cure a thief.

Fear not, you are not a goof
Because tamper-free means open-proof!
Millions try like me and you
Fighting boxes sealed with *Super Glue*.

Truth be known? Bet you'll agree
Today's packaging is a conspiracy.

Those Merciless Meters

Heard that advice again today,
"Why not retire and walk away?
You're getting slow and mighty old
It's vacation time, so go on hold."

A sound theory...yes indeed,
A welcome release from a provider's creed,
But...there are still duties in my care
Meters running everywhere.

Obligations that need put to bed,
A full-time partner not easily shed;
Those meters follow me to home and work,
An efficient and silent recording clerk.

They even run when productivity's dead,
In business we call this overhead!
They may be just and due and fair
Yet overwhelming for a man to bear.

Meters show no mercy, yield no hope,
And add penalties when you can't cope.
Sooner or later, meters take control
Worse than a bank, they mortgage the soul.

Insurance...taxes...utilities,
Licenses, interest, even calories,
Inventory may be out of sight,
Yet those feasting meters still take a bite.

Even when sleeping I cannot escape
Constant calculations —I'm going ape!
As for property meters, in time it proves true
What you once owned, now owns you.

Little chance they will go on hold
They only speed up as you get old.
No escape! They fill up each day
To keep meters running, you must pay!

Don Aslett

The Past Is Past

Must I venture into the futile task
Of trying to alter what is past,
"If I knew then what I know now"
You bet I'd change my life somehow!

Different routes would be pursued
More love and risk, less attitude.
I'd stop the wastes of yesterday
And spend less time in trivial play.

But my course now stands as history
Plus all the regrets that helped mold me.
What's done is done, why replay fumbles?
Just look ahead, avoid future stumbles.

Those old wounds that ran their course
Should now only be a wisdom source,
For I know more now than I knew then
So change today, not where I've been.

If granted reverse, old events could relive?
Chances are the same response I'd give.
So let it go! Things done or not
Don't rehash injustice in every thought.

Let no "would-have-beens" get in the way
And crowd out the glory of today.
This lesson learned from what's gone by,
The Past is past....so let it lie!

Senior Center Scenes

Hi there! You think you know me
As a withered man who can hardly see,
Might perceive cause I limp and use a cane
That playing Bingo is my final game?

Let me tell you a thing or two...
The fun we have here, you've got no clue!
Some of us can sing and others hum;
It's our musical geriatric gymnasium.

Our entertainment might be out of tune
But we croak out songs all afternoon.
Words can change each time we sing a song,
And no one needs perfect pitch to belong.

Don't need a mansion to have a good time
Secondhand is sacred—tattered no crime.
Been here so long I'm almost a renter
Proudest member of this senior center.

Some think it's where they pasture us
When we can't drive a car and must take a bus,
Deemed best place to keep us off the street,
A rendezvous where old duffers meet.

Pensioners, patriarchs, grandparents galore
Married or single? No one keeps score.
Don't have stress over what *might have been.*
Senior Center friends are like next of kin.

No one is vain about their hair or their clothes
Don't care if wrinkles reach down to our toes!
And no wasting time in front of a mirror
Silver and grey is the color scheme here.

We don't buy clothes of the latest rage,
And we're way past fudging about our age.
Too wise to be fooled by worldly façade
Can joke about who'll first be under the sod.

AARP member, but still in there kickin'
Find pleasure in a plain ol' piece of chicken,
Have just enough teeth to enjoy some steak
And we're okay with a small piece of cake.

We dine on old tables missing some varnish,
Good eating requires no title or garnish.
Simple luncheons with nothing to annoy,
Single helpings are enough to enjoy.

There's a spark of kindness in every eye.
About sex and weight there's no need to lie,
We have lots of mileage, and so far no stroke,
A perfect place for the rich or the broke.

So praise to this dwelling's great inventor
Whoever started our official senior center,
Drop by and you'll happily be admitted.
Find out for yourself that we're not baby-sitted.

Don Aslett

Time For A Change?

Call it perhaps...a mid-life review
To stop, measure, maybe renew,
When get-up-and-go begins to slip
And we begin to lose our grip.

We'd like to stay the course for a last hurrah
But our sanity is approaching the final straw,
Life seems weary from stretch and tear
The fabric of hope, almost threadbare.

Painfully surrendering "might-have-beens"
Letting "never," and "if only" win,
Regretting affections unexpressed or loaned,
Risks and adventure too long postponed.

Once we'd bleed for any prize
Our mindset now is compromise.
Time for escape to something new
Get in charge before it gets to you!

Need more savor for a worthwhile day
To shove all the trivia out of the way,
Let's all do better and walk the talk
Because we're running out of clock.

The Weeds Won

A closeness to gardens since my birth
Formed a kinship with me and earth
That fertile ground, from youth to later,
A connection between me and the Creator

My own acreage...I dreamed of it!
One big parcel I did finally get,
Had much privacy and fertile soil
I loved to cultivate, tend, and toil.

Built fences, garden plot, and trees
Mother Nature owned my hands and knees,
For sixty years, sure had my slice
My farmer genes, content, suffice

Fun years of setting tomato tents
And ever battling the elements
Cleaning the springs and dragging hose
Crawling up and down those rows

Toiling through stickers might be hard
Worth one serving of fresh Swiss chard
It was all part of nature's cost
Dodging gophers, wind, and frost

But now too tired to weed and mow,
Rust claims my shovel, rake, and hoe
Weeds and thistles never quit
Free of rodents? I'll never get.

As time and efforts begin to wane
All this acreage seems insane
No time to harvest, no help around,
Carrots and spuds froze in the ground

Ended, my years of a garden fling
Now feel I can't conquer anything
Maintenance is no longer play
Birds and bugs now have their way.

Time to back off? Admit enough?
Enjoy the place back in the rough.
Plant a smaller patch? No indeed!!
Tradition rules, as does greed.

Give up? No...here are my terms:
Next year I'll lick the weeds and worms.
Who knows—at 90, in my garden pants,
I might give that ground a second chance.

Don Aslett

Try On Trial

Try settles for effort not success,
An empty word meant to impress,
Try is dressed in a clever disguise
Waiting in the wings to apologize.

Try is safe harbor's anchor plan,
One of best pretenses known to man,
A favorite phrase, an old Bromide,
That weak and wimpy, "Well, I tried."

Try gives every promise doubt
Providing a clear surrender route
Try makes outcome wholly unclear
Was never uttered by a pioneer.

Try to be faithful to your mate,
Try to eat healthy and watch your weight
It's what we say to avoid a firm goal
Like the boss who tries to make payroll.

Is there try in the Commandments of the Lord?
Do we try for a house we can afford?
To more firmly conquer obstacle's hill
Replace "I'll try" with a marked **"I will!"**

Don Aslett

The Lazy Man's Prayer

Lay I in bed, a morning gray,
Reflecting on what needs done today
Overwhelmed...but accountable...
Many tasks seem insurmountable.

Glassy-eyed at the ceiling I stare,
Seeing barriers everywhere.
All that effort...I must expend
And how much more? When will it end?

I can't face it...me, oh my...
Just as well lay here and die!
Ambition soon I hope will come...
I feel content to be a bum.

In a prone position I get depressed,
Lack the gumption to get up and dressed,
I should be grateful to be alive
All I lack is a little drive.

Can I be cured of this dawning woe? Yes!
Get off my butt, get up, and go!

Rescue Me!

Your search for rescue overdue?
The world has been unkind to you?
Need some help? And you confess,
It's really time for an SOS.

Last of the ninth and running behind,
No good fairy has been assigned,
Lonely, hungry, and kind of sick,
In debt, depressed, on addiction kick?

Out of options and in a stall,
Angels you can't text or call,
Lost and bleeding, sure a mess,
Any savior would need GPS.

In life's trenches, no copter in sight,
Not even surgery can make things right.
Rent and light bill now overdue,
No tax refund is coming through.

What's the program to save the day?
911, are you on the way?
"Daddy? Mommy? Government's hand?"
As you sink fast in life's quicksand.

A sure rescue plan—here's what to do
Need to pull off a big *switcheroo*!
Get off your behind and start uphill,
Start your morning with an "I will" pill.

Action's the answer, that's the gist,
Start with what's attached to your wrists.
Notice how quickly your trouble melts
As you work to champion someone else!

Don Aslett

AMBITION

Life's Bone-yard

Last evening I ventured past
A field where abandoned machines were cast,
Blending into the landscape now
Old planter, mower, disk, and plow,

Among the past where nostalgia breeds
Laced with cobwebs and stealthy weeds,
Worn and broken, weak and blunt,
Replaced by technology's ever-moving front.

Long they functioned, well they pleased,
Faithful engines now fully seized
Still poised for action, just in case,
Their years of service can I erase?

In the backyard of our future dreams
We've oft set aside the "old," it seems,
Until later... awaiting a better fit
Or a convenient time to fully commit

How many well-meaning plans are parked
With a destiny uncertain marked,
End like corpses of wood and tin
Never called to work again?

Affections shelved are now asleep
With promises it's too late to keep,
Thank you's waiting for a better slot,
Kindness left in mind's burial lot.

Hope, like wheels stuck in dry crust
All await freedom! Rescue we must
Make the time, necessary burdens carry
Don't leave action in intent's cemetery.

View Of Do

There seems to be a lot more   *gazers*
                                       appraisers
                                       Hell raisers
Than there are   **trail blazers**!

Lots more   *advisors*
                                       criticizers
                                       uprisers
Than there are   **enterprisers**!

And surely more   *observation*
                                       procrastination
                                       expectation
Than there is   **perspiration!**

Rise and Shine

Morning can bring an empty dread
When doubt and dullness lie ahead,
No worse deal does someone know
Than all dressed up, no place to go.

Absence of a future plan
Limits the venue in life of man,
If not in charge, it's easy to see
We've turned things over to destiny.

Life soon loses all its splendor
When the future we surrender,
Days become an unstructured route
If we let our tomorrows fizzle out.

Motivation, be it so true
Hinges on our looking forward to—
Good portion of faith must be infused
For what's uncharted ends up unused.

No need to chart our eternity
Just daily causes for you and me.
If faith and courage are to survive
Mankind must keep hope alive.

So be not robbed of the anticipates—
The chance of arrival for what awaits,
There's a reason to jump out of bed
When meaningful plans lie ahead!

Get Rich Quick

Tales that impress me less and less
Are all about "overnight" success,
Where business grows with little strain
A miracle or two giving instant gain.

You'll often hear the "millionaire" story
Being one of luck and financial glory,
But things seldom "fall" into place
More often it's a falling on your face.

Rarely come those whopping breaks
Instead it's trials through countless aches,
Plenty of risk and loss of sleep
Enough injustice to make one weep.

Onlookers ought to read between the lines
Where progress has setbacks amidst deadlines,
And grueling decisions over selective deeds
It's seldom realized how a rich man bleeds.

Well known the fetters and sting of debt
And how more familiar the critics get,
Successes others seem to get
Are more likely gross, seldom net.

Before you covet or even believe
The wealth that people actually achieve,
And to keep your conclusion from being wrong
Replace "overnight!" with "all night long."

Don Aslett

Closing Shop

Seems right the effort and intent
To set up an office, shop, or tent
And become an entrepreneur
Investing and committing to endure,
Put hopes and dreams on the line
Open doors, hang "OPEN" sign!

Risk comes with business, one will find
Since economics are less than kind,
In the best of times some markets slip
Like finest corsets and buggy whips,
Be it abrupt, or a slow fade
Some ventures never make the grade.

Appears a condition operations dread
When things go from black to red,
Results— a business's toughest call
When sales and profits slip and fall,
Reach the point where things get tough
And our loyal customers are not enough.

Then comes an action mighty sad
We start throwing good money after bad
Delay and take a few more hits?
Or is now the time to call it quits?
Hang on to that downward spiral?
Before abandonment, one more trial?

Apply new measures, plans, and ploys
When merchandizing favors the bigger boys?
When closure beckons and nothing fits
Go frantic with a rescue blitz?
The owner finally comes to realize
Even perfection can reach demise.

This is not a failure as oft supposed—
Owner's worth remains when the doors close
Honor those who put all on the line
For in life there comes a closing time
'Twould be called bravery by those who know,
The Britts say it best..."Good Show!"

The Entrepreneur's Personal Ponderings

Am I so focused on a single strand,
I'm blinded to the rest at hand?

Is my speed, which is too slow for me,
Excluding dear ones I seldom see?

Is my focus insane in a nonstop chase
Where all my doings become a race?

Always taking on and tackling more,
And looking hard for another door!

Willing to work in snow and rain,
Pushing to progress through praise or pain.

I fight off emotions that might soften me
Does this dam off the flow of sympathy?

Am I so wrapped in praise and power
I think only of the mission and not the hour?

Are the daily victories I find splendor in
When by others viewed, insanely thin?

Because I am always in risk's headlock,
Am I perhaps selfish with the clock?

Are they right? That I'm spread too thin,
Trying to crowd too much in?

Burning the candle much too fast,
Predictions of doom, I'll never last!

I find peace in the survival mode
And pleasure speeding down "challenge" road.

Don Aslett

Help For The Boss?

"When the cat's away, the mice will play"
Is especially true at work.
A worker might stray, on an unwatched day,
And have a tendency to shirk.

But be advised...the boss is wise
And knows what's going on.
It's not a network task, nor does he need to ask
Who's doing right or wrong.

He has helping hands from many little bands
On scuttlebutt's daily trails;
All those rumors at large get to the man in charge
For there are numerous tattletales.

He knows what's cooking, without even looking
He "feels" the hits and misses.
Pettiness of any sort, he gets ample reports,
Who's stealing tools or kisses.

He can read the signs between the lines
Of who is late or early
And how you came to work today...
Cheerfully or surly.

The classified on shelf, he keeps to himself,
Tallied to one side of your score,
Don't have the illusion he can't reach a conclusion
The boss has resources galore.

Don't wave goodbye to what you sneaked by
Good chance it has been recorded.
But bosses let slide much you may hide,
And you'll seldom get reported.

But...don't get excited if you're not invited
When promotion heads your way
You can be sure you'll answer for
The missteps of yesterday.

Genuine Entrepreneurs

Who may wear this title of entrepreneur?
Few qualify, to be sure.
Is it wearing a "business owner's" hat?
No, anyone with some ambition can do that.

Pure entrepreneurs work day and night
Because they think they are always right.
A sacred calling? It's self-ordained,
They're so obsessed, it's seldom explained.

Absorbed in duty to a point diabolic
Way, way past the plain ol' workaholic
Ignoring failure is a standing rule
Setbacks are converted into fuel.

Bravery past the "ol' nest" egg
They'll groan and scramble, but never beg
Always pledging heart and soul
To some seemingly elusive goal.

No reason to stop for a mealtime plate
So few of the clan are overweight.
Exhausted or weary, slow not their speed,
Cost and weather get little heed.

They run free, but keep the rules
Get by without the latest tools,
Fly well by seat of the pants
Unafraid to take a chance.

Often on the edge of debt and starvation
And it's always next year for a vacation
Single-focused, they tromp on toes
And tolerate critics who stick in their nose.

Banks will avoid them, some friends will flee,
Takes years for a tiny profit to see.
Is there a finish line? They'll never tell
And "budget's" a word they can't even spell.

Into the world of maybe's they dive
Wondering why others work only 9 to 5.
To any sickness they seldom yield,
If there is fear, it's well-concealed.

Why do they seem to never tire?
Because they transform duty to desire.
If reverses are looming, they're last to admit,
The real entrepreneur knows not "quit."

Don Aslett

Inventory Reserves

Be thou wise, and oh, so cunning
To not give out while in the running;
Fate takes over when reserves are low
If shortage rules, then we don't grow.

Out of paint, the whole job stops
Out of wind, the sails will flop.
Out of gas, wheels don't turn
When oil is short, bearings burn.

Out of space when clutter sprawls,
If faith is gone hope also falls,
Out of cash poisons any mood
Man turns animal when out of food.

Out of ammo, armies retreat
Out of a job, it's to the street,
Out of excuses makes us lame
Daylight gone, call the game.

Out of matches, campfire's cold
Neglected chores, the farm is sold,
No matter how well you plan ahead
Cutting it close is a gambling dread.

Inventory suffers when in haste,
Essential extras are seldom a waste
The best way to save a wanton hide?
Learn to err to the generous side.

Be wise when you make that list
It's best time to be a pessimist,
Better to over- than under-assess
Running out sure stops progress.

Rah Rah

Signs and slogans, cheers and codes
About good service by the loads.
Standards posted all over the place
And mission statements in your face,

Clever badges, bright uniforms,
Seminars to attitude transform,
All this verbiage makes me nervous
If there's decrease in customer service.

My Shadow

Yes, my shadow belongs to me
No detective trails more skillfully.

He calmly copies all my acts
Instantly! And leaves no tracks.

I can't shake him, Oh, I've tried!
Any misstep, he's at my side.

Mimics every move I make
Asleep is the only leave he takes.
I label him a kindly friend
So agile, quick he does attend.

He doesn't have to say a word
All my speeches I know he's heard.

Reminds me to live free of scam;
I cannot outrun what I am!

Don Aslett

That Bit Of Blind

That little patch of darkness
We all surely possess,
Lurking within our being,
Always present, more or less.

Be it by choice or genetics
Glitches seem to dwell,
A little prejudice and pettiness,
A twinge of larceny as well.

A sprinkle of jealousy and covetousness,
Some insecurity to relieve,
Those second-hand perceptions,
Or revenge we must achieve.

There are blanks in the big picture,
Like a stitch of bigotry,
Where bias still holds its place
Woven in our history.

With our games of blindfolds and blinders
We compensate for all our lacks,
Trust our vision to emotion,
Tolerate envy's cataracts.

We accept the slightest dimming
Into narrow-minded mental trips,
Toying with dusk and shadows
In the path of a full eclipse.

Sad when they take over,
These blind spots we hold out,
Till finally our self-drawn curtains
Become a full blackout.

Measuring Up

We like to strut the tales we spin
Loud and proud about our discipline,
But what of our actions when all alone
When spouse is gone and kids are grown?

No matter how we sneak and hide
Very seldom do deeds stay inside
They burst the seams of our private wall
Our souls reveal and tell it all.

Any scheme we might have cooking
Waiting for time when no one is looking—
How is our conduct when we're apart?
That tells the truth—what's in the heart.

Only in private do we show our stuff,
Like a soul on display in the buff
True character's naked when backstage
Each life becomes an open page.

When our doings risk no penalty
Comes the final measure of integrity.
When doors are closed and lights are out
Then we know what we're really about.

Don Aslett

Covet Stew

We are never satisfied, by heck
Because we always stretch our neck,
And that view of what another owns
Puts green needles to our bones.

For what we have within our nooks
Never measures up to how "theirs" looks:

He makes more money on the job,
His kids mind better than our Bob.
Their pets shed no specks of hair,
Their two-car garage has room to spare.
That man of the house is oh so kind,
And the wife is sexier all the time.
In drought, it still rains on their yard,
His ground is soft, was never hard.
Their cars run better at any age,
Their pictures appear in the lifestyle page.
Their plants are greener, so nursery fresh,
Their long vacations just seem to mesh.
They lounge in back, never tense,
No one's ever sick across that fence.
They inherit money in figures six,
And they can diet, just for kicks.

Their hair stays just the way it's combed,
There isn't a restaurant they haven't roamed.
Their water tastes of the finest wells,
And of chlorine it never smells.
Their stereo has a classic sound,
And roaches are never seen around.
Their place never seems to need some paint,
And the mother-in-law is a hallowed saint.

A waste of life, all this "covet stew,"
Cause they are thinking all this of you.

Hypocrisy And Who?

A well-known character we might fit
That double-dealer called the hypocrite
All the action in pretense based
Can be summed up simply as "two-faced."

The "religious person" we are first to nail
To test their standards we never fail
But don't all of us fudge a bit
Falling short of the Holy Writ?

Hypocrisy can be so well disguised
When any principle is compromised
Speaking with a forked tongue
Whether we are old or young.

It's any use of flattery
Insincere affection to any degree
Truth or facts exaggerated
Standards over or underrated.

A no-no or two— just had to try it
Even most committed cheat on a diet
A major favor that never gets a note
Critical of government yet never vote.

Exaggerating our competitor's tiniest lack
Talking behind our neighbor's back
Using "too busy" for a social escape
Passing the blame if caught in a scrape.

When we utter "no" and then give in
Our conduct has a political spin
Thus in that gap between say and do
Take a look...it could be you.

Conscience Duels

Abundantly rich, yet not content
How useless the emotion spent
In fertile brains we mischief conceive
And soon good sense takes its leave.

Obsession leads to this universal find:
What we dwell on is real in mind,
Be it white lies or fabled crime
Thoughts eventually claim their time.

What's tended in heart begins to brew
And soon enough—the follow-through,
When fantasies are often rehearsed
They imbed too deep to be reversed.

Hard to escape from what mind conceives
We soon answer for the mark it leaves,
Fantasizing erodes values intact
Excessive dwelling ends up an act.

Me Tree

Most any tree, wild or tame,
The finest sermon can proclaim
If man could just as honest be
To bend with injustice as does a tree

A tiny seedling, enough a start,
Then self-sufficiency plays its part
Elements many with time enroll
Rooting deeper, tree wields control

Growing useful without fanfare
Unlocking seasons to freely share
Assaulted often, still survives
Fires, beetles, and insect hives

Chips and bumps of life it takes
May yield a bit, but rarely breaks
Limbs torn off, bark worn thin
Bravely it grows back again

Like finest steeple or strongest mast
Stands as a sentinel when storms are past.
May we when challenged do as well
Once planted on life's hill or dell.

Don Aslett

On The Fence

When it's time for you to make the call
Do you take a stand, or do you stall,
And waver in decision's path
Fearing the critics' aftermath?

Halting awhile to figure things out,
Listening for that seconding shout,
And measuring how the crowd will vote
Or what the latest pollsters wrote?

Is undeclared your point of view
Until you know what others will do,
Too timid to consider dispute
Because your cause might get the boot?

Far safer position is speculation,
Let another make the declaration.
Does group opinion tie your tongue
And all your choices remain unsung?

It's sad to yield to popular sway
When you have your own piece to say,
In the end you didn't make a choice
You're just marching to another's voice.

Don Aslett

Who's The Driver?

So...life is handing you a rotten deal?
Whose hand is on your steering wheel?
Are your gears in Neutral, Park, or Drive?
Who sets the time to depart and arrive?

Who selects the fuel grade and adjusts the speed
And schedules the service when in need?
Who must read the warranty pages,
Is smart enough to read the dashboard gauges?

Who accelerates...controls the brakes,
Selects the road your auto takes?
If the interior is not up to par
Whose drinks and trash left in the car?

Dirty windshield—distorted view
These conditions are controlled by you.
Who reads the signs and shifts the gears,
Honks the horn, adjust the mirrors?

Who puts the day on cruise control
And decides to run on empty or full,
Which roads you will climb or coast,
Picks the passengers with you most?

Regular checkup so you won't stall
Insurance limits? You make that call.
Your journey's outcome—crash or survivor,
It's quite clear: YOU are the driver.

Fit for Use?

A lesson from life's fix-it page
Don't label things useless because of age.
There are many degrees of abuse
And it's your call what is "fit for use."

The ugly, the old, the worn or rough,
If it functions, perhaps it's good enough.
A little slower...maybe awkward too,
But if it works, then it really might do.

Perfectionist demands often get in the way
Such expectations can cause delay.
Not up to par? A mite threadbare?
Bless any spare that gets you there.

As function far surpasses looks—
A blemished bookcase still holds books,
There's life in sandlot's stained baseball
And love for a child's well-worn doll.

A dirty coat tattered and old
Can do a good job keeping out the cold.
Good manners still work in unstylish suits,
Man filled with joy can dance in muddy boots.

Mismatched socks? No cause to grieve,
If you must, can wipe nose on sleeve,
A little spit flattens down stubborn hair,
The ground is sufficient when there is no chair.

Time reads the same on battered clock,
An unpainted fence still holds the stock,
Don't let wilted put things on hold,
Old cheese is good, scrape off the mold.

An old car will often run and run,
A dim flashlight sure beats none.
Slightly broken, blind or lame?
Those with guts stay in the game.

A missing tooth? Needn't starve or beg,
And hands work fine with a broken leg.
Somewhat shaky or some memory lapse?
Most prized quilts are made from scraps.

Lord pity those who demand the latest
When second-hand may be the greatest.
Take pride in patches, have faith in rust,
Utility, not polish, is what to trust.

Don Aslett

Refine Or Decline

In the crowd, I looked around
On both sides of average, this I found:
One man was tall, straight, on track,
Another shrunken with stooping back.

Same were they in age, no doubt,
Both dealt with challenges on life's route
Why the difference in stature, pray?
Did they not live in a similar way?

Heavy loads leave some shoulders strong
But crush others, so what goes wrong?
Survival sharpens the man out front,
The other it grinds to dull and blunt.

One becomes poised in presence and power
The other shrinks, dreading each hour.
Though life dealt equally to both these men
One built outward, the other caved in.

Will the weight and pressure of Earth's dirt
Strengthen us, or cause us hurt?
We respond to events with a smile or frown
Will it build us up, or cut us down?

Missing Out

So sad the treasure you didn't buy
And opportunity passed you by,
Stood in line but missed your turn
Watched your chances crash and burn.

Something you were bent to try
Got just a glimpse when it whizzed by,
When the greatest deal fell in your lap
You were guided by caution's map.

Perfect pose, but wrong lens on
By next day the bloom was gone,
Ripe fruit also has its day
Wait too long and it's thrown away.

Too bad to lose your place in line
Or arrive at the door to a *Closed* sign
Many times there are tears and sorrow
When a job is put off until tomorrow.

Didn't respond? A little too tired?
Too bad, that offer has expired,
Too often life will give you less
If you don't respond with timeliness.

When the ball lands in your own court
You can't score if your shot is short,
You'll never buy if you refuse to bid
Nor taste the food unless you lift the lid.

Oh how much of life is missed
Delaying just to avoid a risk.
Whatever it is that you await,
It's pretty dumb to procrastinate.

Don Aslett

Your Slipping Is Showing

Let's consider—it's not small—
The difference between slip and fall:

The "fall" gets headlines, not the slip
Failure is a gradual loss of grip

Memories slip...and profits too
Slips of the tongue will undo you

Diets slip as most habits do,
"Falling off the wagon" is seldom true

Slow and easy comes apostasy,
And no one "falls" into bad company

Surely one of the saddest slips
Is that of great relationships

You slip not fall into dishonesty
Same pattern for infidelity

You don't fall out of favor or into sin,
Rome didn't "fall;" it slipped within

Slips leave no bruise, a silent mark,
The light that dims before the dark

So don't ignore that gradual slide
That turns life into a bumpy ride

For long before the dreadful fall
The smallest slip begins it all.

If for a saner life you seek,
When first detected, fix the leak!

Boulder Blindness

We fear and fight life's boulders big
That threaten or block our way
Intimidated by these mighty rigs
That loom to darken our day.

But really should we let those stones
Of giants slow our pace
Strip living of its pleasant overtones
And cause wrinkles in our face?

For items large are easily known
We can simply walk around
And when they tumble toward our bones
Their size shouts a warning sound.

It's the little stones, the gravel,
That really takes its toll
Though "harmless" it can unravel
And doom a lofty goal.

In gravel we can slowly sink,
In gravel we can spin,
In gravel we sideways slink,
In gravel we lose skin.

It's the little lies, the little ties
That block us and beat us down,
Not the boulder of scary size
We fear and dodge around.

So dodging bullets of cannon size
Is not your worry, man.
It's the "pingers" that will hypnotize,
I warn you that they can.

So look not just up, but down
In each day's steady tread,
It's little things that break your crown
Not big blows to the head.

Don Aslett

Doing It Over

Might I venture into that useless task
Of reviewing and altering what is past?
That "if I knew what I know now"
You bet I'd change the past somehow!

How strong is history with second chances
For financial blunders and defunct romances?
Be it a minor neglect or a selfish sin
I'd really like to do it over again.

Often have I made that list
Of "do it over" for what I missed
Oh yes, if awarded a fourth strike
I'd curb my ignorance, live more Christlike

Restore time lapse that disappeared
Take more risk with what I feared
I'd keep a better journal and medical health
Address virtue more than wealth

More time with children I'd arrange
Some diet discipline I would change
I'd plant my trees further apart
All improprieties I'd never start

The ball games I lost and plenty more
I'd change my temper, not the score
I'd stop the waste of yesterday
Give less allegiance to trivial pay

I'd shed behaviors that carved out shame
And wrongs outgrown I never overcame
Why, if dealt a second chance
I'd not give sin a second dance

But over is over, done is done
I've concluded life is no practice run
Perhaps with Diety's loving grace
I'll be granted some options to erase.

Sigh! A lesson learned from what's gone by
The past is past...do we let it lie?

Some past is lost, but it's not gone
If one has faith to carry on
Changing things I can today
Covers many regrets of yesterday.

Clearing The Air

In our debates whether God exists
Is one miracle you might have missed
In answer to "Is He really there?"
Stands evidence: Something called AIR!

A stronger foothold of faith not found
What AIR supports! Just look around.
You can hear it, feel it, taste, and smell,
Remains unseen but serves so well.

Air carries sound, directs the rain,
Nurtures plants, and feeds the brain
Birds and planes, it keeps in flight.
Feeds growing plants day and night.

Marvelous power when pressurized
Always available and well disguised,
Useful when pushing out a sneeze
Propels romance with the slightest breeze.

Moves oceans, mountains, and alters lands
Carries frostbite to our human hands
Clouds and thunder cued by air
Can easily sweep vast desert bare.

Though easy to harness or pollute
Man has found no substitute.
There is no prejudice in air we claim
We all breathe and feel it the same.

It's non-selective, rich or poor,
Evidence of God, need we more?
What else must the Creator do
To make believers of me and you?

So in that quest for miracle or sign
Take a deep breath...you'll be fine.

Don Aslett

Life Alignment

The old car would not hold its course
It veered just like a runaway horse.

Unsure of steering on every curve
 I'd hit the brakes and car would swerve.

At any speed got "shimmy and shake"
Holding firm caused hands to ache.

All four tires were nearly bare
Needed more than one good spare.

Then passed a sign: "Alignment Here"
Did a U-turn when all was clear.

Pulled into the shop, process begun
Each car problem soon was undone.

New tires balanced, aligned without force
This fix-it garage is one I endorse.

My life seemed not to be on course
It wandered, swayed by any force.

I gave up reason and what to serve
Lost my way and lost some nerve.

Slithering low like a venomous snake
Life summed up to "gimmee—take."

Gone was my purpose, grew less aware
I was wearing thin, too tired to care.

Then came a prompting crystal clear—
"Make things right in your own modest sphere."

Squared my dealings until I knew
All things wrong in my field of view.

Aligned my actions with a higher source
A price worth paying to get back on course.

In Our Weaker Moments

Life's weaker moments do arrive
When a temptation comes alive,

When reactions generally rule response
And basic needs yield to wants.

At such moments love can be blind
Same as when sudden wealth we find.

It can happen when we're overtired
Also when we've just been fired,

Likely, too, when we're depressed
And especially when we're overstressed,

When bills are piling and our credit's gone
Or a harmful flu keeps hanging on.

Soon more woe distasteful brings
As all mankind does stupid things.

So...Back off, please, and walk away
Weaker time has a huge price to pay.

Don Aslett

Some Risk Regrets

A fellow rehearsing where his life had been
What he would change if it was done over again,

Said, "I seldom ever showed my face
Or ventured beyond the commonplace,

"Safe harbor caution was my game
Rocked no boat, nor wave overcame,

"When chances came for something new
I wouldn't stick out my neck an inch or two,

"The desire and capacity were always there
But for outer limits I didn't dare,

"I stayed on the ground, never out on the limb
But I'd hold the ladder for her or him,

"I took no chance of being liable
Nor sought learning beyond my Bible,

"I protected my station on the job,
I was willing to march among a mob,

"I'd give advice...then disappear
Cause I always had to protect my rear,

"I wanted cushions, afraid to try,
Because risks belong to the other guy,

"Ah...what's gone is gone, and all forsaken—
My only wish is that more risks I'd have taken."

Who's The Author?

When to vice or misdeeds we go
Such a poor excuse, "I didn't know,"

The slightest ding or moral mess
Requires individuals to transgress.

For any misgiving or deed X-rated
Was much earlier contemplated.

We deem ourselves temptation cursed
Though our misbehaviors are well-rehearsed.

Blame sin on fate or that usual "they"
Or on conditions in "this world today."

With more temptations going on
We stockpile excuses for doing wrong!

That big neglect or smallest lie,
A venture we just had to try.

Sin's ownership is no surprise
As lingering guilt so testifies,

Man clearly chooses his own misdeeds
Neither tied to race nor religious creeds.

So...next time you fall... or slip
Remember cause is within your grip.

"Performance" has an author, that is true,
Which author just happens to be you.

Don Aslett

New Car Fever

Matters not the funds or season
New car fever blots out reason.
Fight it? Man, don't even try,
When "new buggy" bites, you will buy.

Time is right for the best of deals
When you "deserve" a new set of wheels.
You're halfway sold once on their lot
Impressive cars like your friend just got.

Rows of beauties! You begin to sweat
Just looking! Haven't decided yet.
How does anyone even stay alive
Without the latest all-wheel drive?

The sounds and looks are oh, so nice!
As you override pleading and spousal advice.
Take a look at that Star Wars dash!
Five more places to stuff and stash.

Better gas mileage would sure be nice
And promises they'll beat the sticker price
With 6-year financing and custom plates
All paid off when your last child graduates.

Further resistance soon relaxes
Final assurance that you'll save on taxes
How vanity turns up the final heat
Once you sit in the driver's seat.

Finished looking! It's buy you must
Transportation has now turned to lust.
Hypnotized, you buy new tech and styles
Though your present car has
            another 200,000 miles.

No payments for a full 90 days,
Zero interest, and you're due for a raise.
Only rescue for car fever in town
Is a car wash with the windows down.

CLOTHING

Wrinkle Worry

What are those little creases
That come on clothes and skin?
Surely a few folds and puckers
Don't constitute a sin.

Twenty minutes spent ironing
Or throwing makeup on—
Who cares about a few furrows,
Should well-earned grooves be gone?

You find some laugh lines over
A really joyful face,
Other sags and corrugates
Just mean you're in the race!

Why conjure up some worry
About a wrinkled brow?
Crow's feet show some wisdom,
And who sees stretch marks, anyhow?

Age earns some body wrinkles
As do our working shirts;
If a sag or two comes into sight
Tell me what that hurts?

Anyone with a pulse
Will have some lines and crinkles,
But who wants to stop a busy life
Over some stupid little wrinkles?

Don Aslett

Waist Waste

In pants, jeans, or slacks, the buggers,
There is a new fashion called hiphuggers.
Sweater, blouse, or fake-fur pelt
Yanked past the bare hangover from a too-low belt.

Throughout day the wearer is pained
Fighting that half buttocks not contained,
Sitting down or getting up
A flash of flesh will erupt

So grab some cover from a blouse
Give dignity to us in the house.
Even if modesty is not the goal
A lot of time is wasted trying to hide that roll.

(G)loves

One of my seldom-mentioned loves
Is the blessing of a good pair of gloves.
They shield and safeguard man's bare hands
From cold, abrasion, wind, and sands.

Like a good pair of shoes upon the feet
They cushion 'gainst friction, shield from heat,
Guard us from what hands shouldn't touch,
They're an extra skin, these friends I clutch.

In my youth gloves were mighty rare,
Father wore the only leather pair.
Our hands were too small, we were told,
Instead got mittens when we got cold.

Without real gloves for chores and plans
Blisters and callouses blessed our hands.
We got a canvas pair in early teens
For picking spuds and weeding beans.

Then that glorious moment arrived
Real grown-up gloves, no more deprived,
They made work easier in those days
For hauling rock and bucking hay.

But no pocket seems able to hold two gloves
No matter how deep or hard I shove.
One slips out, and the time will come
I eventually end up with only one.

My pattern each time a glove is lost—
Into a bin with *single friends* tossed.
If mate is found for a glove so stranded
Why are these twins always *left-handed*?

As life goes on, spare gloves keep emerging,
So this dejunking guy keeps on a-purging.
My years have given me to understand
A glove's best home is on each hand.

Don Aslett

Sandal Scandal

I gave you a chance, you rubber tuggers,
Never again will you be my foot huggers.

No speed of change can justify
The agony you've caused this traveling guy.

I've cramped my toes for a tighter grip
To avoid losing you on a walking trip.

With no protection, I've stubbed my toes
And collected pieces of all that grows.

That open top just welcomes soot
And who really wants to view a bony foot?

I'm sick of your drag and noisy flaps,
The scraping shuffle from those plastic straps.

Today is the end, I'm through keeping tabs
On you miserable, cheap, slippery slabs!

I feel no remorse tossing the losers,
It's not my style, these floppy cruisers.

A Notch Above

A facet of dress not highly prized
Ever see a belt advertised?

This ignored workhorse so well placed
Holds bulging belly or dainty waist

So unnoticed, it's almost sterile
The most functional of all apparel.

If you lose or forget that midriff strap
You'll then appreciate its wardrobe wrap

Replaces the scales on a diet watch
Accomplished by a single notch

Such control of blouses and shirts
Not to mention trousers and skirts.

This quick addition to the daily groom
Takes no space in the closet room

With age it gets better for sure
In time it fits your body's contour!

CLOTHING

Don Aslett

CLUTTER

Souvenir Madness

To any trip we add some cheer
By taking home a souvenir!

Be it paper, plastic, foam, or tin
Can hardly wait—where to begin?

Enough stuff offered to bring one to tears,
Everywhere a bonanza of souvenirs.

Collection fever does commence
For that bonafide travel evidence.

For tiny print on a $5 shirt
$34.50 doesn't seem to hurt,

Customized cup and matching plate
Will it remind, or resuscitate?

Trinket jewelry, never touched by a smith
Means more to people than who they were with.

Now we must fit it on a shelf or wall,
Might even wear it by next fall!

**When we can't remember what it's for
Time to toss it out the door.**

Don Aslett

Christmas Blights

A wreath on the door once kept score
Of who most had the spirit
Now it's a war, to have more,
My neighbor wins? I fear it.

Let it be with one Christmas tree?
Naw...that ain't near enough!
We need bells and lights with shimmering sights
And lines of blinking stuff.

Colored candles on door handles,
And plastic "noels" fake,
Senses dimmed by all eves trimmed,
Like a Mafia birthday cake.

Costing more than nickels, all those bright icicles,
To drape our poor abode
From the roof to gutter, oh it makes me shudder,
This tinsel by the loads.

Wrapped in the bushes and on donkeys' tushes
Are miles of extension cords,
Santa Clause and reindeer paws,
The spoils of Christmas hoards...

Windows smeared, snowmen weird,
Houses like a neon sign,
Colors clashing, Baby Jesus flashing,
30 wise men in a line!

We now contract out this cosmetic route
Just to up a neighbor,
Who breaks a leg from the rooftop crag
During his light-war labor.

Does whole neighborhood look that good?
Methinks we've lost our grip;
This gleaming wonder, what a blunder,
Belongs on the Vegas Strip!

Over-offered

A sure thing in human destiny
Is that over-offered we will be,
Too many proposals our whole life through
Endless options to preview.

Solicitation comes in different ways,
It appears 3000 times a day
To try, to test, to drive, or wear
Miss a deal? We wouldn't dare!

On sale or discount, we must concede
Marketing convinces us what we need.
Then our good sense fully off guard
Gets an eager accomplice—the credit card!

Already so much is on our plate
Can't savor what we accumulate;
So it's unwise to get so excited
Buying every item we get invited.

Instant message, Facebook, and Twitter,
Consume our time with computer litter,
Banner ads for quick promotion,
Bandwagon buying creates commotion.

Samples offered, some are free
But obligated we should never be.
Don't listen to temptation's voice
"To buy" or "to pass," is still a choice.

Life's best moto? More is less.
Stay away from the spiral of excess.
Let's quell that lust for ownership
And live free of the creditor's grip.

Don Aslett

Un Clutter

The question was, "Do they have as much
As we in the US of A?"
The junk and clutter piled askew,
Just *STUFF* that's in our way.

All I can tell, as I travel well,
Only here do we have the room,
In Japan each house has maybe one fan
And only a single broom.

In our dwellings fair, we have room to spare,
Even a second place,
While living quarters south of our borders
May be smaller than *our* closet space.

Here in the States, we collect plates,
And display them just for mood
Other countries compete for something to eat,
Their focus is finding the food.

In Himalayan hills, they find thrills,
Carrying goods in small back pouches,
While we rent storage for extra lamps
And for our outdated couches.

Arabs move about, and well make out,
With nothing but a tent and camel,
We live clutter-deep with extras heaped
And all kinds of fine enamel.

China makes more junk than can fill a
    pirate's trunk
From morn' to late P.M.
Why glory be, they are clutter free
Because we buy it all from them.

Our collection spree in the land of the free
Soon made us the land of MORE
Now a world leader in clutter, too—
The proof is inside our doors.

What Is Enough?

In this life we've always tried
To vault somewhere past satisfied.

Life is full but "could be fuller"
Perfect! But we can add more color

Friendship deep, but could be deeper,
Package nice, but not a keeper

Salary high, but could be higher,
More benefits and early retire

Not content with riches galore
We dream, we seek, for a wee bit more

Maybe it's greed, would you agree,
Wanting that land that borders me?

Past good sense we often trample
While we're living well with ample.

Even though our stomach's full
We eat until our senses dull

Our solution when feeling sad,
Another something we must add

Anxious to gather...we don't know what,
"Compounding" merits a further glut

How much more must fill our tent
Until we reach that "I'm content"?

Don Aslett

Luxury Losers

For opulence, I'll make no claim
Or participate in luxury's shame
Where misspent money and emotion
Reeks with the scent of lavish lotion.

Social climbing that squanders wits
Excess consumption that never quits
Is what we drive or how we dress
For beauty? Ego?...anyone's guess.

Incessant shopping through the door
A trail of trash from vanity's store
Adorn ourselves in awkward gowns
Cosmetic ourselves into painted clowns.

Embarrassing, these wasteful sprawls
For aimlessly wandering through the malls
Resources squandered on lavish whims,
High maintenance pools for infrequent swims.

Shows of grandeur as splendor's host
Where wisdom surrenders to glamor's ghost,
Seven-course dining claims table position
Where garnish and frills trump sane nutrition.

Luxuries whisper, "Better than thee,"
The quiet foreplay of prosperity.
Escape this environmental and social abuse?
Ought we live simple "fit for use?"

Bird feed

Near alley dumpster the birds soon found
A half spent pizza on the ground
Sprawling scraps of every size
Lots of crumbs and one large prize,
A full slice indeed, a weighty lift
All intact—a foremost gift.

The mightiest bird snatched that slab,
The remaining shreds did the small birds scab,
A modest taste for smallest of flock
Content, each one, with crumbs off the block.

But that mighty bird straining its neck
Spied a tiny bird nibbling its peck,
Dropped the slice, flapped over to seek,
And seized the crumb from the small bird's beak.

What others have seems so prime
From winning the lottery down to a dime.
Discontent, though our plate is full
The want for more has terrific pull.

Even when we're over-blessed,
We seldom pass this covet test
Greed or pleasure, we use our might
To tyrant the lesser, cultivate spite.
**Let's leave other's goods alone
And feast on what we already own.**

Don Aslett

Free Lunch

You've all seen bug zappers, electric trappers,
For insects, mosquitos, and flies,
Attracted at night, bugs swarm to the light,
Then drop dead with fizzling cries.

Dwelling nearby, with a glint in his eye
Perched a gecko, wise beyond (lizard) years,
Who found if he stayed, by the light where they played,
His dinner freely appeared!

Such a sweet deal, this pre-cooked meal!
So he camped out there every night,
And snagged every fly, as it fell from the sky
His system was stress-free delight.

He sure had it made, there in the shade,
But his scheme soon came to an end,
Because without any cares, on one of those snares...
His tail did overextend!

His bottom all fried, the gecko soon died
Because he never looked around
Nor felt indebted; just entitlement fitted
As he slipped into burial ground.

So much for free lunch, it cost him a bunch
The outcome proved quite tragic.
When you have a plateful, best to be grateful
Because nothing appears by magic.

Winged Cure

Tired of depression and daily strife
I launched pursuit to change my life!

First I dodged some deadbeat friends;
Found avoiding people rarely mends.

Next a visit to my shrink
Left feeling quite the same (I think).

A college class: Psych 101
Taught stress results from what's undone.

So doubled my work but all I got
Was fluttering heart and stomach knot.

Tried reflection and pious prayer
Still couldn't shake my deep despair.

Maybe a pill will make me numb?
Addiction risk was way too dumb.

Took up exercise, ran hardcore,
Went jogging past a *Pet Smart* store,

I stopped to stroke a dog and ferret
Left that shop with a speaking parrot!

Took him home, set on a perch...
Soon would end my depression's search!

For the wise little parrot, true to his name,
Whatever I said, he repeated the same.

If careless words I did not delete,
The mimicking bird would quickly repeat.

My recorded voice throughout the day
Was exactly what his beak would say.

Alarming the verbiage from that bird
Echoes of my own mouth heard.

Remarks I made with no one around
That parrot copied to later expound.

His pounding chatter helped me conclude
That I, not others, set my mood.

And so my winged pal brought me to grips
That mental condition starts with my lips.

My problem's internal, not bad luck or "they,"
But of living the action from words that I say.

So any of you on depression's trail
I have a secondhand parrot for sale.

Don Aslett

The Flea And Me

Across my windshield a flea did race
Twice frisking past my face
I might have smashed that little pest
And ended his survival quest.
Instead I rolled the window down
And sent that flea out on the town.

It may seem quite a peculiar stance
To give that bug a second chance,
But age has my compassion won
Life is precious once begun,
And to kill unnecessarily
Is a most unpleasant task to me.

To all you bullies on a trophy quest
And yobs who fell the robin's nest,
Poor and senseless blood that's spilled
For entertainment lust fulfilled,
Is all sense lost in that "sporting" box
Like hunters and hounds after one little fox?

Nature's harvest, be what may
But ugly act when we kill for play.
No deep feelings when causing pain
Is a loss of love in heart and brain.
Value of life should sharpen with age
For all that moves across life's stage,

I know not the feelings of that flea
Only how good his escape felt to me.

Squirrel Savvy

A system based on reality
Kind of a squirrel's mentality,
Where those who are young and able
Work to sustain their own table.

Self-reliance, it is called
Each owning what they've hauled,
Some extras for their young and old,
Inventory when times are cold.

In this stash of worker fill
None is there for Loafer-ville,
Why should idlers get to eat
Spending time on butt not feet?

Should others work off their bushy tail
Supporting those who choose to fail?
Storing not while sun is out—
Fellow squirrels rescue? This I doubt.

The system's called pay-your-way,
That's how squirrels spend their day,
Their example we should emulate
A behavior we could promulgate.

Don Aslett

A Mountain Lion's Life

Ever have those days of high demand
So business traffic weary
Where mind and body becomes unmanned
Every emotional fiber dreary.

It's then in the mid-afternoon
When we slur our very talk,
We long to stretch in the warmth of June,
Like a cougar on a rock.

We'd crawl out on that sunny ledge
Where the sun might strike our pelts,
Make ourselves a relaxed wedge,
Loosen tie and belt.

Then with the sound of the creek below,
Breeze whispering through the trees,
Half close our eyes, let drowsiness grow,
And restore our well-worn knees.

Ah-h, to be finally curbed, yes undisturbed,
Snuggled on that jutting cliff,
The P&L can go to hell
Won't answer a single "if."

Insects buzz away as we lazily lay,
Nestled like a rug,
Flex our paws, relax our jaws,
And give ourselves a hug.

Let schedules sail, as we twitch our tails,
And nap a day or two...
If you feel the same and need a break from strain
Bet there's a place for you.

A Case for the Quarry

READY!

If you want to see good sense depart
Watch man go ape when "the season" starts
Be it for spirit or macho display
They're out to blast some poor critter away.
Go forth mighty hunters with hairy chests
Full throttle on some trophy quest.
Not for defense or survival he finds thrills
Chasing innocent quarry all over the hills.

AIM....

To outwit the prey, careful to manage
Big money spent for the hunter's advantage
They struggle out of a Cabella's store
With trinkets, ammo, and gadgets galore
Wear the scent, imitate the call
Must get a trophy for the wall
Isn't there a hint of ridiculousness
Adorning self in full soldier dress?

FIRE!

Hunting, yes, is here to stay
But how about sporting fair play?
There must be some governing code
Besides shoot, shoot, shoot, then reload!
If the game travels on foot, so should we
No horses, trucks, or ATV
If the beast gets the hunter, all is fair
Then let's chalk one up for the bear.

RETIRE

Thus ends my verse, be not I sorry
To make a defense for guiltless quarry,
Might we question man's good sense
To pay for "sport" at a life's expense
Shouldn't events we label sport
Keep our contests on turf or court?
Of these magnificent animals running wild
How do you explain hunting to a child?

Don Aslett

Defining Smart

In a sincere quest to define "smart"
Is there an accepted place to start?
Many mapped courses...I suspect
Most connect with intellect.

Those who can recite and memorize
Surely earn some public prize.
Perhaps the ones who get straight "A"s
Will get their share of mankind's praise.

Those with an MBA or PhD
Do have some smarts, don't you agree?
Smart at chess, win spelling bees,
The strong in faith, with well-worn knees,

Honor to them who will keep a job,
The pure who never cheat or rob,
Those immersed with self-reliance
Or understand all rules of science,

Leaders who lead from the heart,
Talent that turns skills into art,
Those who conquer being deaf or blind
Show evidence of a greater mind.

As our composite wisdom does increase
Will it get smart enough to install peace?
And will our ever-expanding brain
Have sense to come in out of the rain?

Topping all definitions we might bring
Smart is doing the right thing.

Don Aslett

Schoolhouse Surprise

The old schoolhouse held a small surprise
As students spied with sleepy eyes,
A small bird perched, with a blinking stare
Trapped up high in their classroom there.

Delightful screams caused instant fright
That startled creature then took flight,
Airborne and darting as birds will do
To a spot where light was shining through,

Only to crash with a sickening thud
Window marked with feathers and blood.
Back and forth it repeated this drill
Falling limp again to the windowsill.

The more battered the little bird became
The more determined his freedom to gain.
He could see the sky and trees and grass
But couldn't get through the invisible glass.

There seemed no rescue—bird was too high
With all this pounding it surely would die.
Then teacher entered and bid class no fear,
Opened high window for escape free and clear.

Alas, the bird stuck to its route—
Same collision results! Would he ever get out?
Finally it followed the entering breeze
And found a pathway to sky, grass, and trees.

It soared in large circles, in winging parade
Wonderful freedom! A right choice was made.
Like this bird we all mimic so well,
We crash and burn under habit's spell.

Our energy spent in bouncing off walls
Full-time recovering from all our falls,
Repeated wounds, little time to heal
We start over again, our hopeless ordeal.

Because life at times is equally cruel
Confining us to our "stubborn" school
May we, this small bird's lesson learn
The source of freedom for which we yearn.

Impertinent flights and harder course
Wear us out with continual remorse,
Look to the Master who does arrange
An open window for us to change!

Diploma Delusions

In cap and gown I cross the stage
I'm 18 now and fully of age.
Soon as that diploma's in my hand
I'm more entitled in this land.

No living cost, thank the Lord,
As I still have free room and board
There's an extra car for me to use
Any family trips I get to choose.

I can romp at many a spree
There's a janitor to clean up after me.
Yes, right now I don't need to plan
Cause there's a cell phone in my hand.

For Daddy's lawyer can clear my failings
And Mother's doctor mends my ailings
Can go to college for eternity
There are scholarships galore for me.

Study? I won't have to sweat
Because I have the internet.
No need to think or plan ahead
I can use job benefits instead.

If these resources get sick of me
There's always a benevolent agency
And if my funds are carelessly gone,
I have welfare to fall back upon.

If I get lost in life's parade
The government will always give me aid.
If when older I've an empty plate
To the rescue will come my parents' estate.

****

Yes, out of school and on my own
Must pick direction now I'm grown

Could slide into that "dependence" slot
Or develop the skills I've been taught

Put action to art, math, and science
And pursue a life of self-reliance

In cap and gown, I've crossed the stage
Will I serve mankind and earn my wage?

Don Aslett

Payback?

Oh, how it makes such little sense
To learn at someone else's expense,
Good is help to get you through
But what is the moral thing to do?

First, a handout is kind of dumb
If you don't know where the support is from,
Before the school you are attending
Find whose money you are spending.

Whether donors be rich or poor
There are principles one cannot ignore.
Somewhere funds are earned or saved
Someone worked and someone slaved!

But glory, glory is the day
When someone shows up to pay your way!
A politician's dream—education free!
For the able-bodied how can that be?

Your education is not finished yet
Graduated? You may still have debt!
You own the degree, now you owe
Those who financed you to grow.

Smart enough for scholarship track,
Be smart enough to pay donors back,
A sponsor's earnings passed on to you
The same for others you should do.

Remembering Recess

Rushing to my next enterprise
A familiar clamor I recognized,
Over there on the grade school grounds
'Twas recess time; I knew that sound.

That frantic burst to get outside
The race to monkey bars and slide,
Where instant games emerge at will—
Unnoticed goes a scratch or spill.

A blend of screams, laughter, and shouts
Innocent gossip, and wrestling bouts.
Brief freedom from academic drill
Precious moments of playground thrill.

To feel the air, touch lawn and trees,
A long-awaited break from those ABCs.
Bad weather? Who takes heed?
Space is all the children need.

Teachers cast a kinder eye,
Minutes seem to flutter by,
Time's too short for a bully's rule,
Classroom clown now less a fool.

Recess time so schedule-free
Enjoyed with such sincerity,
Now I long for that recess bell,
An agenda rescue from clientele.

Please fifteen minutes to help me heal,
Liberation at the school-bell's peal,
A welcome pause from corporate drudge,
Litigation, money, and things to judge.

Still I'm waiting for that bell to ring
And free me from the boardroom zing,
Replay good memories a second time,
And leave behind this corporate climb.

Don Aslett

Give Up Or Give In?

For all that "too much" on your plate
Is there a time to capitulate,
And let those hopes and dreams of old
Slip away and slowly fold?

Time, money, or maybe age
Tears out aspiration's page,
Reserve resources running low
Survival signals it's time to let go.

Now thrusts forth from vision's grave
That white flag you'd never wave
Releasing something from its place
To a someday time we all must face,

Sacrificing that might-be chance
Like selling off part of the ranch,
Shifting dreams to a slower speed
A loss of virtue? Yes indeed!

What more can cause a heart to bleed
Than that old option to concede—
Giving up what we lived to fulfill,
Content to take some lesser thrill?

So what is it that makes us stay bold,
And keep juggling more than we can hold?

Don Aslett

Snuggle With Struggle

If I started retrenching because my gut was wrenching,
I'd become a worthless wimp.
If I let myself skid for a drooping eyelid,
I'd start seeing my spirit go limp.

If I altered my course, for every charley horse,
I'd have regrets by the ton.
If I lost enthusiasm every time I felt a spasm,
Nothing would ever get done.

If my clock ceased to tick because I felt sick,
I'd never get out of bed.
If I gave up the tussle at every sore muscle,
How would the family get fed?

If I demanded rest, every time I'm depressed,
I'd become a total loss.
If I stopped when I'm tired, and whined to be fired,
I'd be my own worst boss!

If I was fear infected every time I was inspected,
I'd be a sniveling paranoid.
If I gave up gain, every time there's a rain,
My net worth would surely be void.

So if you find a struggle, don't cry, just snuggle,
Use each setback for a stepping stone.
No use to holler, you'll grow taller,
While building a firmer backbone.

Quack Grass Lesson

As a professional landscaper I stopped to gawk
At a busy old man crouched on a walk
Who was digging away at a concrete crack
Pulling out quack grass–a hopeless task.

Stubborn roots, resisting his will
That man stayed focused on weeding…until
He slowly looked up as I stared down
And cried, "That stuff is all over town!

"You'll never get it all; your time is squandered."
He nodded his head, words briefly pondered,
And through toothless grin made reply,
"Though my days are few, I can still beautify!

"This task will take a full three or four days
But friend, the result will merit much praise.
As I pull out stalks and roots, one by one,
I can touch the soil and feel the sun.

"My shaking hands are not good for a lot
But this sort of work I can do while I squat!"
A flood of compassion enveloped me
At this well-taught lesson on dignity.

With many weeds in my character's path
Like judgment, impatience, and plenty of wrath,
This was a reminder–a message divine:
Weakness is tackled, one root at a time.

Don Aslett

A Bit of Larceny

Oh, curse that bit of larceny
We all have in our souls
We're 99% honest...but
That 1% sure pulls.

Willed to a path of moral-hood
We strive to do what's right,
But slip past all those minor things
When we think we're out of sight.

Just to gain that inch of ground
On the darker side of sly,
If no one has to suffer
How can it be a lie?

"Advantages" more than deserved?
Might tip into our favor,
A little unearned praise or cash
Is what we seek and savor.

Perhaps it's just a "one up"
By means inflationary,
Grabbing for the biggest piece
We view as customary.

Oh, curse that bit of larceny
We all have in our souls
We're 99% honest...but
That 1% sure pulls.

Don Aslett

Getting Even?

Some minor injustice you can't let be
About some trivia you cannot agree
Reach a point, "can't take no more!"
High time to even up the score.

So you find yourself in get-even mode
Choosing revenge as your mother load
Participate in centuries' old fight
Trying to make two wrongs a right.

They hit you? Gotta hit 'em back
Even a small trespass—you attack!
So keeping revenge hatefully fresh
You live to get your pound of flesh.

On vengeful path to return the pain,
Accomplished! Tell me, what did you gain?
Why do you bristle and stay alert
Demanding justice for the smallest hurt?

Futile this wound you determine to chase
Afraid to let go and simply erase
Once eye for eye, now it's the other cheek
Aggression surrenders to the meek.

Takes real courage to suck in and adjust
As for revenge? Backing off a must!
Pay the "fine," take the lumps,
Tolerance is solution to all life's bumps.

Free Ride

We always get a secret thrill
When someone else foots the bill.
A sure freeloader's warning sign—
Can't distinguish your dime from mine.

When the other guy pays, is it not strange
How taste moves above its normal range?
Be it someone else's bucks
Our choices move toward deluxe.

A chance to freeload, most will grab,
Let Daddy Warbucks pay for the cab.
Just fasten on the moocher's bib,
Skip the hamburger and eat prime rib!

There is added thirst at an open bar
Fudge an upgrade on the rental car
It's a staggering plate at the buffet
And some for home gets tucked away.

Out of my pocket? I'll pass up dessert,
But on your tab, it just won't hurt.
For that bill on the restaurant trip,
If company pays, do a bigger tip!

When lying on that final slab
Expect someone to pick up the tab?
The subtlest test of integrity—
How different we live when things are **"free."**

Don Aslett

Genuine Germs?

Missing work while being paid?
In what drunken stupor was this rule made?
Is this little extra of employee care
Compensation for not being there?

    Perhaps "sick leave" has been misnamed
    When missing a full day's work is claimed,
    Sick means hospital or home in bed
    Not a chance to go shopping instead.

The perk is there and seems to say,
Find an excuse to call in sick today?
To miss work, find a darn good reason
Like tooth abscess or H1N1 season?

    You have a sore back or ache in the head
    How many farmers are "off" sick in bed?
    Life has injustices, its share of glitches
    Champions work on in spite of stitches.

Holidays and sick days blend together,
Understaffed or under the weather?
Amazing to see how "sick leave" pays
For hunting trips and golfing days.

    Miraculous recovery when sick pay ends
    Their medical history they quickly amend
    Seems ailments' severity, to my dismay,
    Hinges on what "sick benefits" will pay.

So use caution before walking that line;
Make sure your germs are genuine.
Maybe this practice should come to a halt,
Why is your illness the boss' fault?

Live Haggle Free

A chiseling game of subtle duress
Where two parties bargain more for less
Be it for properties, time, or wares
Looking for bigger slice of shares.

So goes the waste of negotiate
Where integrity can slip to exaggerate
A parley to squeeze your fellow man
To get last inch or penny that you can.

Character must be pushed aside
And any honor slips to pride
To take any advantage that you're able
And leave no excess on the table.

How can any victory abound
In beating a brother's value down?
If willing to accept less than you ask
You're only absent a robber's mask!

How far will each party need to go
When honesty only takes a "yes" or "no"
Should matter less who's lost or won
Set a fair price and call it done!

Don Aslett

Snake Oil

There's a smooth operator to beware
You'll find him lurking everywhere
Clever as he might be sly
Still he is easy to identify.

A slippery character we all know
Who can sell ice to an Eskimo
And toss in a Brooklyn Bridge or two
With perfect "deals" cut just for you.

Knows well the angles and politics
An expert at bribes and plausible tricks
Lacking not in wit and charm
Eager and willing to sell you the farm.

He conceives, contrives, consorts, conspires
Any "confidence games" he inspires
Promises speed and shortcuts galore
Can get you in at the ground floor.

Knows well the skill of dangling carrots
Living high on others merits
Another's funds he's quick to exhaust
Logics you into footing the cost.

The "American trust" he will pledge
And push the system to its legal edge
Oh how many he will fleece
Always steps ahead of the police.

General prey is someone they know
Like friends or family who have the dough
So for those "deals" that too oft go wrong
Say a quick "no thanks" and move along!

ETHICS

To Catch A Thief

It was never a part of my belief
That "I" could ever be a *thief*,
But in the many faces of *larceny*
Participants we all might be!

Perhaps a type of *robber* was I
When stopping my child's right to try,
Or bribing my kid for better grades,
And excusing his wild escapades.

Dismissed his duty, I confess
By cleaning up a teenager's mess.
In giving him unearned allowance
His thrift and drive I did unbalance.

Robbed another's time by being late,
Shorted tithes on the church plate,
Clearly one plays the *bandit's* role
When able to work but on the dole.

An insurance question I refused to tell
Took a sick day when completely well,
Did personal duties after time card punch
Extended my eating at noonday lunch.

Padded expense account that I was sent,
Surely a form of *embezzlement*,
Company tools at my home are seen,
Did personal printing on an office machine.

One might label it a petty *crime*
To text and call on company time.
When leaving the building, yes, it's true,
I did grab an extra pen or two.

That extra income, did I report?
My per diems always come up short,
Withheld another's well-earned praise,
Cooked the books to get a raise,

Bounced a check knowingly,
Fudged a bit on that warranty,
Then gained Advantage, pulled my rank,
Defaulted a loan that hurt the bank.

Left my mess for others to clean,
To dodge adult admission, posed as a teen,
Aware of a deal that was corrupt
Knew justice, yet did not speak up.

Never returning a borrowed item might be
A perfect example of *piracy*.
Even supposedly honest person me
Does things that could be thievery.

Don Aslett

Exempt?

Do we perceive and start to believe
That rules are for other guys?
While they shouldn't cuss, it's okay for us
Cause we see them through different eyes.

And when we slip with tongue or lip
There is always good reason why.
With all our flaws, we're above the laws,
That only to others apply.

Such as caution signs and speeding fines
Exempted, we presume,
Tough regulations that govern the nation
To them we are immune.

Whatever will be won't happen to me
I'm free to tread in life's garden.
Others misstep. Me? Never inept
For my stumble there's always a pardon.

It is error indeed to think we won't bleed
If we start to believe we're exempt,
For we all win or lose from how we choose
The outcome we can't prevent.

Ignore building codes, increase roof loads,
They will fall on us...kaboom!
Crowd the borders, ignore the orders?
That's orchestrating our doom.

So all you bright souls, stay out of holes
And keep the rules, my good friend,
Or you'll get your dues and in the end lose,
For any rules that you bend.

A Real Friend

Steve is my BEST FRIEND

Who dares define companionship?
The bond that eases my life's trip,
That person with a reassuring glow,
Giver of light when my candle is low,

Puts magic in all events at hand,
Energizing what's stalled or bland.
When weariness has too much its way,
A single touch keeps "quit" at bay.

Strengthens values, improves tone
Becomes the soul's chaperone
An aide, a tutor, at every test
Knows my dial from work to rest

Compassion's door will not close
Sorts and serves my wants and woes
More than a mentor, more than a guide,
A supercharger at my side.

Don Aslett

Homeless At Home

A homeless problem is in our city!
We gesture toward the street,
At scribbled note on cardboard sign
Propped against calloused feet.

We cringe at the soiled, thread-worn clothes
The vagrants often wear,
But what of the pain on the tender face
Of a child missing parental care?

Too many kids that we ship and trade
To their part-time ex-mom or dad,
Are more homeless with a hired maid
Than the sign-holding, soiled nomad.

We shudder when we see the homeless
Pawing through a dumpster can,
While we pick up our own greasy meal
At a fast food drive-through stand.

"God Bless"/"Down on my luck"/"Please help"
Each drifter holds his glum sign,
But none is as sad as the well-clothed lad
In a tear-stained Calvin Klein.

Do vagrants lack intelligence
Because they wander so,
Are the "rich" that much better off
With house-stations for stop and go?

There is no place of refuge
Without affection in the home,
Though we faithfully attend our meetings
And take kids to the sporting dome.

Any child is homeless
When love is absent there,
No *Head Start* program compensates
Or even the best daycare.

Home is more a state of mind
Than an address or dwelling place,
And nurturing cannot be shoved
Into a welfare case.

Homeless them or homeless us
We observe in summary,
Are these begging street vagabonds
More at home than we?

So let this be a wakeup message
To those who feel security,
Our concern should be directed more
Toward the real-life poverty.

Path for the Kid
or Kid for the Path

When candles begin to crowd the cake
There comes a path each child must take,
In this rugged world to find their place,
Do we prepare them for it, or control the race?

Do we lighten their load should they tire
Or simply hold their feet to the fire,
When their follies in life pile up enough
Do we fix their ills when things get tough?

Is our weaning so long delayed
That self-reliance shift is never made,
Do we protect to the point of overkill
By carrying them up life's tedious hill?

No way will we let the youngsters fail
We're right there and quick to pay their bail,
Let no recess bully lurk around
Or allow their clothes to touch the ground.

Be it any condition they cannot hack
Daddy Warbucks takes up the slack.
For the setbacks and pains that life will bring
Do we call an ambulance for a bee sting?

Must we dictate what they hear and feel
Prevent all blisters that come with the deal,
Can a child cope with bumps and dings
Always tied to parents' apron strings?

For unfriendly reversals that life may spring
Do we steer all choices with tight nose ring?
The path is hard and long and toiling,
But do we help adult kids by spoiling?

Don Aslett

A Child's Tears

A child's favorite weapon to negotiate?
"Turn on the tears" and things go great!
Stubborn outbursts, quivering chin and lip,
The manufactured tears begin to drip.

Drenching cheeks throughout the day
Whether time to get up or to stop play.
Stubborn revolt when cleaning up a mess
Weeping when told they must bathe or dress.

Instant sobbing and distress they feign
Or quickly stop when tears shed in vain.
With that reservoir of tears to get their way
Even sensible parents begin to sway.

Parental "No's" sure lubricate those eyes
Though genuine tears flow at sad goodbyes.
If left behind, how those droplets flow,
Or after bad dreams that in time they outgrow.

Hungry tears manifest with a howl
So does soap in eyes absent a towel.
Crying from an **owie** is usually not fake
Legit tears come from a tummy ache.

But pray a child not reach that barren drought
Of long dammed tears that can't come out.
Unshed tears from adult cruelties
Inflicted too often and carelessly.

Tears from rejection or neglect,
Muted sobs that go unchecked.
Hurts and fears hidden carefully inside
Tears from sorrows never amplified.

Anguish bottled up, the tears that keep,
With buckets of pain they wrestle and weep.
Imprisoned behind their dry-dock bars
Those invisible tears leave the deepest scars.

The Coconut Tree

In youth, I passed by a coconut tree
Oh! Could one be owned by me?
Be it pride or stewardship
My wish turned into ownership.

For a seedling, I paid the price
Read instructions once, then twice,
Gave it spacious growing room
And watched it daily bud and bloom.

In Mother Nature's hands a cinch
That silent progress, inch by inch.
Impatient with its growing rate
Slow, so slow. Must I wait?

As focus shifts and efforts stray
To other things, I turned their way
Then, it happened overnight!
That tree reached its glorious height!

Cursed part of life, the unwatched scene,
To miss what happens in *between*.
That splendor that escaped my view
Those tender years, as it grew.

A child, like that coconut tree,
Nurtured by only a small part of me,
In hands of teachers or peers to train
As trees are assigned to sun and rain.

Blinked one day, and there they stood
Towering in full man and womanhood;
Loved ones blossom on their own
Before you know it, they are fully grown.

Alas, the loss—won't you agree,
How life copies that coconut tree?
So vain are all regretful sighs
And that useless appraisal, "How time flies!"

Don Aslett

Black Sheep Leniency

Rebels! Rascals! Are words we scream
At defiant children gone extreme,
Their venture outside the family fold,
Has broken traditional family mold.

Made a blunder finding their place
Big time stumble, then fell on their face,
Black Sheep label is quickly predicted
As wayward child is now convicted.

Family convenes to save the lost
As image becomes the real cost!
When judgment starts to enter in
Must separate the person from the sin.

We all are misguided, and at times unfit,
As we exercise our misplaced grit.
Oft dims the memory of our early day,
When we might also have lost our way.

Weak isn't wicked, a behavioral flaw,
Let classification be done by the law.
While some delay in their maturity,
Recall that rebellion built democracy.

If the accuser was never in such a spot
It's likely because they were never caught,
**So before we cast that initial stone,
Best review the flaws we own.**

FAMILY

Don Aslett

The Refrigerator Door

In the kitchen of most any home
Is refrigerator door boasting art or poem,
No spot is more sacred for memoirs galore
Than what's posted on the icebox door.

A family creates its own billboard—
Marketing space that one can afford
There's a magazine clip you found darn cool
Posted near a tidbit fresh from school.

Reminders, quotes, photos, and lists,
Schedules coming…and ones you've missed,
A scripture you're trying to memorize
A measurement lest you forget the size.

Genealogy forms you cannot escape
Hung by magnets or old scotch tape,
An appointment too busy now to file,
A cartoon or quip that earns a smile.

Job lists, reports, and dated weekly menu
Starting to overlap junior's soccer venue
Right there displayed in random spread
A family scorecard easily read.

Immaculate homes need a contrast or two
Though kinda messy, this gives a clue
This family scrapbook in constant view,
A fridge door FaceBook just for you.

Baby Asleep

Increased reverence a soul will reap
Witnessing the symphony of baby asleep
No touch! No talk! Armlength's gaze will do.
For just a moment absorb the view:

Invisible breath in a dreamy hush
Uncaptured by photo or artist's brush
Not manifested in the name or clothes
Is the glory in tiny fingers and toes.

Born to either pauper or wealthy prince
Captivating is any baby's innocence
Such slumbering sweetness to behold
Puts all thoughts of trivia on hold.

Are not little ones the pulse of society?
Matters not whose the baby may be,
A radiant bundle in a package of time
That connecting pause to something sublime.

With no higher honor are we blessed
So savor the presence of each little guest
A confirmation is each precious soul
To the purpose of the Creator's role.

Boomerang Kiddies

When the schoolbell no longer rings
Untie that knot on the apron strings—
That time will come, it's hard to believe
Precious rug rats the nest must leave,

To go and seek a life on their own
Leaving tired old parents alone.
For the required journey well prepared
Do they leave confident, or scared?

As life will deal a tougher route
Some tender chickadees might go without,
With pressure when things get out of whack
It's natural to want the old room back.

If any have a homeward track
Darn good chance they will be back,
On their own they ought to be
But why strain, when back home is *free*?

How flawed is love as life is spent
Absent the dignity of honest rent—
Being a resident, not occasional guest,
Robbing parents of an empty nest.

There comes to view a great surprise
That most welfare is seldom wise,
For rarely is there growth or gains
When we replace another's growing pains.

That camel's nose under the tent
Is it parental rescue or entitlement?
In changing childcare to a science
Let us please not rob self-reliance.

Don Aslett

Food Fever

For food and shelter we thank the Lord
But must we feast to overboard?
We seem to have famine mentality,
With our national display of obesity.

It's nothing short of a glutton's wish
To create the most exquisite dish,
Dessert concoction and prime rib to carve
We cultivate waste, while others starve.

Hours wasted on an elaborate brew
When sufficient meal is a bowl of stew.
Sandwich artistry on food channel show,
Shapes of bread from colored dough.

Measuring cups and Teflon pans
Aching backs and greasy hands
Three mixing bowls when one would do
Elaborate settings to feed a crew.

At each event we expect to be fed
Instead of delightful, it's what we dread.
Out of balance, we worship our food
Putting on weight just to elevate mood.

Don Aslett

Where Has All the Flavor Gone?

Perched on top of produce bin
Large and plump with varnished skin
A store-bought tomato, ripe and red
That later proves my taste buds dead.

Lustrous color is feast for the eyes
When did its flavor vaporize?
Resembling nothing I recall,
This red orb has no taste at all.

Faster grown with hot fertilizers
And added preservation's modifiers,
Can we remember what it used to be
When the tomato had an identity?

Cherish the day when friend comes by
Shares garden tomato for me to try,
And Yes! It's what I remember from past
Eyes closed, taste unsurpassed!

I wonder if mankind boasts the same—
Caring about looks and a famous name,
Trying to mimic what others have been
Seeking for image, leaving depth thin?

Pretentious like that red oval sphere,
No substance beneath a thin veneer
Appearance perfect, but contents gone
It's called the *Tomato Phenomenon*.

Oatmeal Inflation

About the recent price raise
I've maintained a polite hush,
But now, I'm not too happy
'Bout the change in breakfast mush.

For the last week in the restaurant
I ordered up oatmeal,
The dish brought to my table
Was a seven-dollar deal.

Twelve bites it took to consume it;
That's half a buck a munch!
Hardly sufficient nourishment
To last me until lunch.

Remembered I the good ol' days
When the price was less unnerving,
Then, cereal piping hot was sold
For less than five cents a serving.

Don Aslett

The Airport Hot Dog

I promised myself that never again,
No matter how desperate I might be
Would I lower myself to the serve-yourself
At an airport eatery.

It was seven years since that last hot dog,
A meal that shortened breath,
But amazing how time and hunger heals
The fear of digestive death.

But two meals I'd missed, and the outlook bad
For food along the way,
It's said every man does have his price,
And this was a hungry day.

I shouldn't have stopped at that grill
Of dogs rolling in shiny grease,
Or noticed others eating them,
None of who looked deceased.

So I ordered up to try again,
A load I'd gulped before,
One more chance, with a nervous glance,
I wolfed down that tube of gore.

Now here I sit, on the verge of tears
My system out on strike
Wondering if in five more years
I'll repeat this Maalox plight.

Buffet Restraint

We may worry about expanding girth
But need to get our money's worth
At this ordered display of tempting food
That fills our gut and boosts our mood.

We lose all markers for portion control
With unlimited food and drink on the dole.
Love every dish, not a single complaint
There's no attempt at buffet restraint.

Pizza to ribs, take all you please
Succulent rolls or mac and cheese,
Buffalo wings, glazed ham and fish,
No need to cook a single dish.

Perfectly arranged, each entrée is great
As I carefully fill up my oversized plate,
Back for seconds, and thirds shouldn't hurt
Then onto fajitas and pie for dessert.

Fresh scones appear, can hardly wait!
Pile those babies ten-deep on my plate,
My buttons are ready to pop, I admit
Need to put down my fork and quit.

I grumble to leave this savory feast,
Another iced Coke to guzzle, at least.
Then to my delight—they announce an award
Just drew my name for a free smorgasbord!

Don Aslett

Serious Cereal

Pick up grocery cart, head for cereal aisle
Mission? Find Quaker Oats, the Old Fashioned style.
Ha! There is the box, though way down low,
In Quaker garb that man we know.

Alone and smiling from the bottom shelf,
"Why wasn't he perched higher?" I thought to myself.
Then a flash of adventure filled my soul:
Was there something better to fill my cereal bowl?

Variations of wheat, bran, and rice came to view,
My choices were exactly one hundred forty-two!
Tony Tiger, Trix Rabbit, and Snap Crackle Pop,
Capt' Crunch, Mickey, and Sugar Bear up on top.

Reviewed all the claims and sure licked my chops,
Grabbed Loops, Charms, and Pebbles, tossed in Sugar Pops.
Finished off my cart with Kix and Alpha Bits,
Cookie Crisp, and Krave—I was on a buying blitz!

Though Waffle Crisp I could barely choke down,
I still tried Reese's Puffs next time I was in town.
Refusing to yield to any diet defeats,
On to Cinnamon Crunch and Frosted Mini-Wheats.

The more kinds I bought and curiously tried
More the waste of half-eaten boxes multiplied.
Hard as I tried to munch and chew,
I didn't make it through all one hundred forty-two.

Enough preservatives added for digestive shock—
Feed dog the contents and instead eat the box?
Perhaps this poem may quell your quest
And accept your old favorite as simply the best.

HEAL✚H

Gurney Guts

At first it is a nagging doubt
Some body parts needed fixed or out,
X-rays and blood tests seem to prove
It's a problem they can remove!

Talk is plentiful 'til the time's at hand
And the final procedure is decided and scanned
Reality approaches once date is set
Will you survive? Friends make a bet.

Panic lies below that forced grin
At arrival time when you check in;
Laporoscopy or large incision?
You sign off to the surgeon's decision.

Insertions, reductions, or biopsy
Fifty pages of fine-print ceremony,
All of a sudden you feel inept
As down the hallways you are swept.

Needles, tubes—it's like a zoo
Green masked ninjas gang up on you.
Then…finally terror gently goes…
Tingling surrender from head to toes.

Before very long you start to "come to"
With alternations done and surgery through,
Blessed relief, the operation's over…
And you escaped pushing up the clover!

Don Aslett

The Wake-up Call

How many wake-up calls do we need?
One or two, we never seem to heed.

First alerts seldom make a mark
As we stumble on in the dark.

Blind or calloused we struggle through
Slow to realize those warning lights are true!

Handicap

"Sad" we say when we observe
One handicapped from birth,
A crooked spine or useless limb
Might label cruel this earth.

But sadder still, are us "fortunate" ones
Content upon comfort's shelf
Having no excuse or reason for disuse
Because we deformed ourselves.

My Primary Caregiver—Me!

As healthcare with *our* ownership starts,
We are the authors of our own patient charts.
The Primary Caregiver should be each of us—
Let's stop throwing our docs under the bus.

In our caffeine-addicted, bi-polar states
Most problems come from overloaded plates.
We abuse our bodies to an addicted shell
Then pay for specialists to get us well.

There is no way our clinicians can win
As they deal with our lack of self-discipline,
These heroes work to delay early graves
Monitoring our pulse and even brain waves.

Wellness is our responsibility, from the start
We are the authors of our own health chart.
How can we hope for the best possible fate
Without giving up habits and losing some weight!

Don Aslett

HEAL✚H

Ahead Of Hippa

A patient's condition, no need to assume,
Gossip starts in the waiting room
They draw conclusions about your case
Just by judging the look on your face.

If they don't overhear, they speculate...
Come up with diagnosis for your fate
Age or accident or body parts failing
Private turns public when someone is ailing.

About others' functions they just have to know
How big and how many pills in tow,
How is the drainage, what's the blood flow,
How many times did you just have to go?

And talk of medical ethics, all that's corrupt,
No matter the condition, someone one-ups.
If your tumor is barely marble size
It's softball size to the waiting room guys.

All visitors discuss your vital signs
And the variance in your oxygen lines,
The pain threshold from one to ten,
And how many tubes the nurses stick in.

The size of the incision, how big the cast,
How long under anesthesia did you last
Everyone can know your ultimate doom
If present long enough in that waiting room.

HEAL H

A Tribute to Doctors

Surely mankind's greatest win
The progress made in medicine,
Faulting doctors makes little sense
May I offer a verse in their defense?

There's a specialist for every body part
From arthritic feet to the aching heart.
Different docs for eyes, joints, and throat,
Fixing asthma, headache, and tummy bloat.

When bodily functions are out of sort
We toss the ball into their court.
We trust the physician knows how to restore
Each problem—so we feel like before.

They may biopsy spots or adjust our back,
Do x-rays, or stents after heart attack.
They explain how to take each medication
For high sugar, cholesterol, or constipation.

With simple words and bedside charm
They describe our condition with no alarm,
Disorders and syndromes, each has its name
Heredity or environment, something to blame.

We rush to them when feeling faint
They address our ills without complaint;
Replacing hip, setting broken bone
They graft, do stitches, add silicone.

Be it cancer, diabetes, or maybe age
They run tests and try to gauge.
If we are victims of overload plates,
Prescription addicted, or in a mental state.

By medical codes each doc is bound
Tolerance for error is seldom found.
Even when we don't deserve to live
The doc remains fully positive.

These "fix me" pros sure get my votes,
All the men and women in white lab coats,
Heroes who delay our early grave
Especially when it's my life they save!

Don Aslett

Cancer's Answer

Once to all disease I claimed immune
Today I sing a different tune!

There came that bullet I couldn't dodge
I'm now in cancer's repair garage.

It moved in on me a while ago
Finally, one day it let me know,

It was indeed a huge surprise
Cancer was for those "other" guys.

Amazing how quick lifestyle can change
Life's hope and plans time to arrange,

What was once so well controlled
For at least a while, big plans on hold.

Forget the worry about high cholesterol
When cancer makes its wake-up call,

New action in my body stirred
Now wearing labels I'd only heard!

Radiation I deemed a heating process,
And chemo, some Chinese woman's dress,

New diagnosis I cannot pronounce
Drugs and tests I cannot denounce.

With pills that exceed the price of gold
More tests coming I've been told,

A new playing field soon to know
Cancer is not a one-man show.

Care extends far past "YOU"
Takes friends, family, and a pro-medical crew,

One big frustration soon to find
A weakened body with an able mind.

Suddenly competing in a different league
A new meaning to the word fatigue,

Of unstoppable drive I cease to boast
An unwelcome villain and I'm the host!

On the path to shed this pest
I must set new records for sleep and rest,

A great pin cushion, I look uptown
Really quite stunning in a hospital gown.

An increase of faith one might observe
Why dealt injustice so undeserved?

Well that's just the way it is, my friend,
Add to vocabulary "treatment" and "extend"

Can't always settle for what is fair
Most of us mature have had our share,

I'd welcome double dose of what I now own
And suffer the invasion without a moan
If cancer could leave small children alone.

The Home Gym

On some machines sweaty people sit
Use weights or jog the path to be "fit,"
Regular life, if given a chance,
Will help you better fit your pants.

Walk or run to work instead of ride,
Get off the couch and get outside,
Mow your lawn and clean the yard,
Paint the place, haul off, discard.

Just tax the body morn to night;
Wrestle the children, a pillow fight!
Clean the house, mop the floors,
Change the lights, refinish the doors.

Build a project with the scouts,
Rescue some local down-and-outs
Move some furniture, the biceps test,
Shoot some hoops, don't stop to rest.

Gardens build a stronger back
Weeding will the thighs attack.
Why to a fitness center must we roam
When bodybuilding can be done at home?

Don Aslett

Take A Walk

Be it for miles, or just a block
Nothing like a chance to walk
Imagination goes into gear
In walking's rhythmic atmosphere.

Walking's a premium privacy
For pondering fact or fantasy
It will work off some of that oversized supper
Replace coffee and the need for an upper,

Give opportunity to clear your conscience,
Beats sitting around on inactive haunches.
"Why walk when you can ride?"
An answer? Just look at your backside.

Though independence it to man will give
This transportation is viewed as "primitive."
Hunters now have ATV's and horses,
Carts save walking on all golf courses.

Luckily some still walk their dog
Sometimes this can end up a jog!
 Want to be a real pioneer?
Then put those shank ponies into gear.

Faster Grocery Shopping

As I walked through the door
Of my favorite grocery store,
For living healthfully I could see
Shopping could much easier be.

Skipping most of the "bad-food" aisles
Would give more time for walking miles,
I wouldn't even have to go
Down that long liquor row.

And there would be no big crisis
Skipping the row of chips and spices
Don't even have to slow my feet
When wheeling by that fatty meat.

Pop and colas only calories bear
The cookies and cakes can stay right there,
Drugs and rubs I can pass by
And exotic foods I don't have to try.

Into the basket, save the tosses,
I don't need those enticing sauces
Best to miss fresh pastries in stacks
And without magazines I'll feel no lack.

Passing up processed food saves the legs
Just **perimeter shop** for milk and eggs,
Grab fresh produce then head on out
We'd all live longer from this healthier route.

Don Aslett

Smug Bugs

Christianity has its characters
And even some nincompoops
But overall good and striving
This awesome, gentle group.

The atheists are okay guys,
They just snipe across the fence.
The fanatics I can also bear,
There're just a bit intense.

The "preachers" are found everywhere,
Aren't all of us part reformers?
To the sinners' club we all belong,
We cut our share of corners.

But it's any who feel they're safely saved
Who think they've gained it all,
Who've crossed a self-drawn, moral line
And assumed some holy call.

They know the answers, one and all,
And have such pious mugs
What is more unholy
Than Christians who are smug!

Don Aslett

Mirror Mirror

The failings we search for will appear
Most readily in a simple mirror,
If someone's flaws the source we seek
Pick up that glass and take a peek.

Victim or villain, therein we spy
Our own reflection does not lie.
The source of outcome, foul or fair
Is found in that reflective stare.

That mirror can pin suspicion's blame
Because it knows its owner's name.
And should we find a no-fault mirror?
Well…objects are closer than they appear.

Gaining Compassion

When daily life seems close to boring
It's time to stop and go exploring

**For abrupt reminder in our stay
How good we have it every day.**

You can't evaluate win or lose
Until you walk in others' shoes.

To appreciate your breathing range
Just run your own errands for a change.

You think your boss has a sour face
Trade work for a while, take her place.

If assembly work seems easy and fine,
Take your turn on the production line.

To comprehend cleaning, do the mopping,
To know stress, the Christmas shopping.

Before you start an environmental bash,
Haul your own garbage to the trash.

Think it's easy to be clothed and fed?
Just cook your own meals and sew instead.

**Learn compassion as a tool and guide
You might end up feeling good inside.**

Don Aslett

A Bit of Soul Searching

A church affiliation I do claim
And the parish records bear my name
But could I be part hypocrite
Who displays, not reads, the Holy Writ?

Do I only trust and call on Him
When faint of heart or weak of limb,
Are my prayers unfocused or in touch
Am I using grace as a cushion or crutch?

In a test of faith will my witness wane
Will the covenants I made need a cane,
Am I evidence blind when hope is thin
With an imagination that harbors sin?

Though I may never use His name in vain,
Do I too often cause His children pain,
Are my beliefs anchored in parental right
My devotion illuminated by borrowed light?

Is church attendance a conscience fix
And holiness hinged on politics,
Could my "reverence" be for the praise of man,
My devotion to duty a character sham?

Might I just be a self-serving sloth
Waiting for prodding by those of the cloth?
Hoping any dark past or sins be waived
Yet knowing till proven, I'm never saved.

Will I hold up when the end is near
Or wash out when I'm faced with fear,
I must reflect on the reserves at hand
How strong a test will my faith stand?

Leap Of Faith

As for that "leap of faith" often sermonized,
That long-jump link to the Godly prize
This goal of faith on pathway steep,
Methinks requires more than a leap.

Faith's price is work and exercise
Spiritual shortcuts are never wise,
Must wriggle and writhe to get us there
With humble tears and repeated prayers.

Takes push and process to shape the soul
Faith comes in portions, seldom whole,
Resisting response to diversions' urge
We inch along, seldom surge.

A barrel of good works we must fill to the brim
A once-jump chance is mighty slim,
Now...no path to faith will I fault
But I doubt the luck of a one-time vault.

Don Aslett

Sneaky

Leave a mess?
Break a law?
You escaped...no one saw?

But! Be advised
All acts and sin
Will always be caught
By the man within!

You pass sentence
Cause you're the judge.
Your dungeon's dug
To the depth you fudge.

Dirt may wash
But filth remains,
And you are the one
Who classifies stains.

The trial and sentence
You self-assign,
Your bars and cell
Are your design.

Stone Casting

Humanity oft travels down a road
Into a frenzied lynching mode,
Rushing to break another's bones
Self-righteous bring the largest stones.

Those stones of envy, stones of hate
Passing sentence on another's fate,
How another's sins come quick to mind
And to our own we are dim or blind.

On hearsay are many cases built;
Perception is evidence for guilt,
Eager take we, the stone in hand
Before the victim takes the stand.

Pre-jury sentence, don't you see
Turning misdemeanor into felony,
A liberty no man should take
Where another's character is at stake.

Accused have rights of privacy
Without input from you or me,
Their reverses we ought to grieve
Never broadcasting what we perceive.

A neighbor's agency must be left alone
Or we are worse than whom we stone,
As all men sin, no boundary sign
Puts all on "stoned" side of the line.

Neighbors' actions are their own story
Let's permanently close our stone quarry!
To condemn, convict, never were we sent
Let the Lord deal any punishment.

Don Aslett

The Bad List

Say some scoundrel
Did us dirt?
Must get even,
Return the hurt!

So we were wronged
Maybe kicked around
Why make injustice
A battleground?

We let a long-past tiff
Build a fence
Or a political difference
Erase good sense.

A bad list exists
Just to keep track
Of those whomever
We must hit back.

The bigger the bad list
The smaller the man
Reviewing the grudge
Whenever one can.

That shameful ledger
We carefully keep
No good benefits
To ever reap.

True forgiveness
Is too late sought
When we bury the hatchet
But mark the spot.

There is a choice
Above keeping score—
Forgive, forget,
Or just ignore.

It takes up space
To house discontent
Revengeful message
Clearly sent.

We pick a side
And never budge
Turning minor glitch
To a genuine grudge.

Once locked in
A biased void
Friendships easily
Become destroyed.

Petty Is Not Pretty

Few lower species can be found
Than an actively focused hearsay hound,
A person with a heartless brain
Who relays gossip on a dead-end train.

Expanding glitches of suspicion
That send us on a shallow mission,
Assembling fragments in a poison brew
Letting biased perceptions pass as true.

Chairman of the false witness club
Trained by demonic Beelzebub,
Fitting oneself in a judgment booth
Taking license to trivialize truth.

A mountain-maker from molehill dust
Defaming others inflames distrust,
Jealousies fuel the insecure
Victims groan and pain endure.

Petty is not a pretty pursuit
And it leaves reputations destitute,
It can't spell forgiveness or forget
But finds cubbyholes for the false to fit.

Someone's more, doesn't mean you're less
So, please no part in pettiness,
In this life let's be sure we find
A way to leave this habit behind.

Don Aslett

Imagination

(in 1st Person)

Hello, old pal! Remember me?
Your imagination is who I be!
I operate in your head all right
With conscience and the Creator's light.

Like a butler for your whims
Available when doubt or reason dims,
For wants and wishes even public made
I'm always willing to come to your aid.

Can reduce guilt, the soul to please,
Best selling author of your fantasies,
I host your world of make-believe
Will take control when morals leave.

Can induce pleasure, joy, or fear
Engage your tongue before brain's in gear,
Provide an escape when life isn't fair
Can enhance joy or cloak despair.

Counsel and comfort, I might provide,
But I do have a poisonous side,
Hard to distinguish between lies and truth
Sad to say, I am not always foolproof.

I flirt with too many might-have-beens
Of business and romantic whims,
Suggest you use some noble sense
To always review my consequence.

In closing, a caution I give to you
What's often imagined becomes true,
So take the time to clearly identify
Whether I'm a friend...or the bad guy.

Imagination

(in 3rd Person)

Imagination, be it friend or foe?
Is a permanent companion, this I know,
Both a judge and jury, our mind controls
Where behavior answers to it's goals.

It functions as a two-edged sword
With capacity to torture or reward,
To be feared or highly prized
Where hate, like love, can be fertilized.

Finding nourishment on slightest doubt,
Take truth or error on its chosen route,
Bonded bridges it can build or burn
Allies to enemies it can turn.

Fulfills all self-directed dreams
Of glory or distasteful schemes,
Taking assumptions that do not exist
Promoting them into an avenger's list.

Once left wondering to imagine the worse
Imagination turns into a punishing curse,
Where reactionary paths prove unwise
And honest emotions are fictionalized.

This paranoia becomes sharpest spear
The cruelest jailer for a man to fear,
Be cautious of its mental sway
Which can grind good sense away.

Imagination is ours and free,
For relief or bondage, what will it be?
That faithful companion is standing by
To rescue or to crucify.

Don Aslett

No Stopping Zone

Once embarked on this public route
No graceful way to simply bow out
On a self-inflicted merry-go-round
Exit from which I haven't found

So many demands I've lost count!
Life at a gallop, too swift to dismount
My daily dashes, now a marathon,
Roadside rest stops, yes, all gone

Too many dependents, I must not fail
No excuse for absence, too busy to bail
Refuse to wear a dropout's label
To admit defeat? Not when I'm able!

Commitments maybe too freely given?
Once the driver, now I am driven
So...who could we seek a notice to give
If we want to adjust the life we live?

Expectation or agency, it's on we go!
For all the blessings we own...**we owe**.

Don Aslett

LEADER**S**HIP

History Before It Happens

So many characters in the human race,
Here is one you may someday face—

These innocent, over-trusting souls
Seldom afraid to share their goals

Who see conclusions before they start
Puzzled when others don't take part.

They rush ahead, giving great offense
To cautious ones perched on the fence

To seek a utopia they madly strive
Keeping idealism in overdrive.

Risk or failure they cannot spell
And outcomes to others they rarely sell

When their clear vision remains unshared
They chant that *others* are vision-impaired.

Short on miracles, no crystal ball
Seldom weigh cost or witness a wall

To logic and reason they can be blind
But in them a core of bravery you'll find.

We may never meet their secret good fairy
Our choice? Help or humor the visionary.

My Critics

Marvelous creatures my critics be
How oft they think and speak for me,
So attentive and never afraid
To mind my business and let theirs fade.

The more I build and serve and try
The faster my critics multiply
They are an efficient bunch
Creating evidence from mere hunch!

To public view, my faults they bring
Can find all manner of mud to sling
These faithful armchair quarterbacks
Second-guess when and where I lack

Such expert shooters from the hip
They can dissect my slightest slip
Latch onto stories and gossip share
Regardless of who was even there,

Taking me places I've never been
While assuming an impending sin,
Diagnosing my actions and my thoughts
Exposing things that I am not.

Even though they're vision impaired
My privacy is broadly shared
By critics unknown to even me,
Thanks for the marketing. And it's free!

Don Aslett

Flattery Factors

You say I flatter? Yes, its true!
I find, then praise, the best in you

If I deem you're worth your name
All your virtues, I'll acclaim.

You may let your talents sleep
Trust me to hail what you won't peep

I'll quickly rip off your disguise
And all your assets eulogize

Every plus in you I spy
I'll enthusiastically glorify.

For what I praise in you doth rate
So why resist when I adulate?

When you find yourself all buttered up,
You'll know you're worth a trophy cup.

Dwelling on the good I see
Will only increase your dignity

Praising you is time well spent
Please accept the compliment.

LEADER SHIP

Role Model Legends

My childhood idols at age fourteen
Both on the field and movie screen—
Cleveland Indians and Brooklyn Dodgers,
Humphrey Bogart and Roy Rogers.

Sought I to be the bravado character
To each was I the silent competitor,
All were Icons of fortune and fame
In youth I hoped to be the same.

My first real love was Doris Day
Couldn't put Lou Gehrig's poster away
Knew Shirley Temple would always be fair
And Jimmy Stewart would never swear.

Red Skelton's show required no bleeps
John Wayne always played for keeps,
Heroes were always caring and clever
I'll remember their actions and voices forever.

Though I never knew and never met
Heroes upon whom my sights were set
Of all our champions from the past
This question is most often asked:

Are there heroes that are down to earth
Where example counts and has its worth?
Do healthy role models exist today
In our community—not in a screenplay?

We may never meet the musician or actor
Or play in the ballpark or become the master,
Yet, for a moment in time let's smell the fame
And follow a true hero's homerun game.

Memories are quiet but deliver a dream
Giving us hope when actions lose steam.
Set our own sights, surrender no goal
We are the actors in life's real role!

Don Aslett

LEADER**S**HIP

Playing The Fame Game

Being recognized or eulogized
Does surely have its price,
You'll learn fast, fame doesn't last
So here is some good advice:

For wealth's acclaim or a big name
You'll need some added endurance
On this depend: "famous" can end
So carry some vanity insurance.

In that bumpy ride, with others after your hide
There's a test of a real titleholder
The limelight has power to sweeten what's sour
For influence to be bigger and bolder.

So be forewarned and fully armed
If notoriety comes your way
Who you really are, a dud or a star,
Is often on plain display.

Some stardom and rank, you can take to the bank
But again we casually mention
There's honor at stake to give, not just take,
When you get any public attention.

There are many benefactors behind great actors
Fame's not a place one can roost
A public post is no license to coast
It's leverage to give others a boost.

If you're really a big deal, the needy you'll heal
Rebounding the praise of fanfare
Everyone knows true greatness grows
In seeking your neighbor's welfare.

LEADER SHIP

LEADERSHIP

The Doer

It's those extra ordinary folks
Who do five times their share
Carry triple the load of others
And still have time to spare.

They run a flexible schedule
Always crowding more projects in
Leaving a trail of accomplishment
Everywhere they've been.

Their drive is seldom for money
Nor do they do it for fame
Wanting to prove life is earnest
Not just pleasure to gain.

Entrepreneur or workaholic?
They treat work as if it's play
Often in their presence
It's easy to feel in the way.

Ever pursuing accomplishment
They appear intoxicated
Sometimes they wonder if they're loved
Or just admired and tolerated.

Often their very presence
Rates a respectable sigh
Some people voice a polite relief
When doers leave or die.

There's fraternal bond with fellow doers
A kinship and a style
Where they meet and socialize
In that second mile.

Don Aslett

Kids' Summer Jobs?

A summer job, are you kidding me?
My kid needs play-ability.

Work can come later, for little guys,
Right now, they need to socialize.

There are lessons, classes, clubs, and camp
To whip this tyke into a champ.

Piano, trumpet, language art,
In all things cultured must take part.

On to yoga's pose and stance
Along with the usual gym and dance.

No better place for self-esteem
Than getting on a swimming team.

Sports and drama camps are there,
Peewee football everywhere.

Buy the gear and pay the dues
Each sport then needs different shoes.

How did great heroes ever open doors
Who spent summers doing chores?

Don Aslett

Out Of Tune

True, some music has its place
But please not constantly in my face,
There's time and season for every taste
But out in public, it's misplaced.

People think it is your treat
To hear armpit music down the street.
Car passes by, windows down,
A booming bass heard all over town.

Everywhere across the nation:
Restaurant, shop, or fueling station,
At travel stops or on airplanes,
Buses, cabs, and even trains.

Waiting rooms and grocery stores
Athletic events, filling all outdoors,
Even on the phone when put on hold
Music repetition sure gets old.

Seems everywhere it's clamor spread
Rap with volume that would wake the dead
Construction job sites, pure disaster—
Every worker brings a ghetto blaster.

Guitars and horns like sirens shout,
Numb-eared say, "Just tune it out."
Beating, blaring, one could go ape
Screaming pounding, there's no escape.

Any music should best interest serve
Instead of shredding other's nerves,
Most of it doesn't make the grade
It's moved from inspire to invade.

To those volume-blasting trained,
Time to keep your noise contained,
Can't we harness volume and tone
Leaving pure silence all alone.

Lack Attack

When I find life going lame
Surely there's a source to blame
My condition just has to be
What society has made of me:

So much fast food down my throat
I.B.S. and stomach bloat
Incredible garage sales every spring
So cheap I must buy everything!
Lost ambition in that fancy spa
That fuzzbuster made me break the law
Las Vegas slot machines, I never win
Those tattoo parlors ruined my skin.
Credit card offers put me in debt
Lower interest will not offset
My genes have made me overweight
Traffic always makes me late.
None of my bosses were any good
I live in a high-risk neighborhood
I'm not responsible for what I did
With abusive parents as a kid.
Police and government are after me
My life misguided by bad TV
There are so many reasons I'm a wreck
Those doctors ruined me, by heck!

When luck wanes and relationships lack,
We search for a scapegoat we can attack.
But when we view it all honestly,
All blame really belongs to me.

Don Aslett

TV Trauma

To relax I grabbed that TV remote;
Fun entertainment was my vote,
Surfed 800 channels with hope sincere
That quality content would soon appear...

Surely on that big digital screen
Worthy programming could be seen,
But every click brought the usual stash
Endless soaps and reruns of M.A.S.H.

Shopping channels full of junk sundries
Aging preachers touting their ministries,
Overpaid athletes chasing a ball
Or how to get rich—by not working at all!

Found 6-pack abs beneath scrawny chests
Parading tight butts and exposed breasts,
Psycho doctors analyzing moods
Thirty-five channels worshipping foods.

Elected politicians giving their views
Candy-wrapper women rehashing the news,
Guns in my face and spatters of blood
Six-in-one tools to clean off the mud.

Cosmetics and pills to keep us alive
Cars and trucks only rich people drive,
Discount insurance anyone can get
How to beat taxes and credit card debt.

Mindless quizzes and reality shows
Drunken people and scanty clothes,
Wore out my thumb; so what is left?
My favorite new channel called...O-F-F.

LIFESTYLE

Adults Only

In our quest to track "evil" down
Don't need to look beyond our town
To find influencers that betray
And hidden persuaders who lead kids astray.

Who buys the tickets to raunchy shows,
Designs and markets immodest clothes?
Who prints cheap rags for willing hands
Makes drugs available on demand?

Who serves the food so rich with grease
Fast food our children to become obese?
Who decides what movies to play
Or passes the sick humor of the day?

It's not youth who run porn shops or bars
Or write X-rated scripts for movie stars,
We moral folk have made the bed
Paved the path where a child is led.

Hunt down those culprits, yes-sir-ee,
Boy, they look a lot like me.

Don Aslett

Hooked On Speed

I wonder in this world of speed
If we get the sense of calm we need

Where went tolerance for slight delay
Has virtue in patience slipped away

Too quick for things to turn about,
No time for goose bumps to break out

Gratification instantly pursued
In a universe of ready fast food

Has patience's fuse become too short
With instant replay in every sport

Speedy delivery, on its way
Get your order the next day

Instant message, instant lift
Instant photos, instant gift

Faster credit, faster pay
Faster service, shorter day

Quicker muscle and body tone
Instant text on any cell phone

Meds for quicker pain relief
High speed "tech" to make things brief

Has excitement lost its place
In the constant hurry of our daily race

Blotting out joys of anticipation
Shorting the needs of imagination

Overriding savor, letting time fly
While too much grandeur passes by

Keeping Score?

We've found ways to measure any feat,
Packaged so we can "compete."
Be it fair, good, better, best,
Somehow we can't let it rest.

Whether we are rich or poor
We're always looking for a score.
Measurement comes in degrees
So faster! Faster! If you please!

More muscle or a better pill?
We take competition to overkill,
Converts innocent fun to being "best,"
Pulling every talent into a test.

"First place" becomes a predator
As play-yard fun now needs a score.
Neighborhood skateboarding just for fun
Has now become an Olympic run.

Once hunted and fished for food and pleasure,
Now for trophies that we can measure.
Competition thrives like the devil
As play is taken to a "professional" level.

Usually the "loser" we find
Is only a fraction of seconds behind.
In any competition that we choose
Even bad teams win and good teams lose.

Back home, when children's games are done,
Parents' first question is, "Who won?"
Oh it makes so little sense
To let scores or points rate excellence.

As stadium fever continues to gain,
Have we not become a bit insane?
Must keep tabs on this effort spent;
The bottom line—it's just an event!

Don Aslett

LIFESTYLE

A Gift Shift

Few acts convey a better lift
Than exchanging the well-timed gift
Each person plans just what to deliver
Which blesses receiver and the giver.

A doorstep basket without a name
A load of wood for fireplace flame,
Love and kindness well conveyed
But has *giving* become overplayed?

Turning service into a chore
Most have plenty but still want more,
A mountain of pressure that leads to debt
Figuring what to give and what to get.

Was gifting easier a few years ago
When needs were great and room to grow?
Once satisfied with a stocking filled
Our image now must be thrilled.

Through websites and stores we bleed
Weighing what fellowman might need
Cards or calls are simply not enough—
We must add some bulk with other stuff.

Emerson has it well summarized,
A *portion of self* is thrifty and wise;
Unmatched, the best gift from you—
A sincere visit would nicely do.

LIFESTYLE

LIFESTYLE

Values Gone Wonky

Noticing measurement for who's highest paid,
Sadly found in spectator-ing, not in a trade

Necessary professions merit little attention—
When was last time plumbers got media mention?

Food and shelter should be the first two
Next, transportation and health would do.

But that's not their fortune—who gets it all?
Athletes who kick, throw, bounce, or catch a ball.

The other group to which economy bends
Is paid millions for prancing in front of a lens.

For media icons or whoever competes
We'll buy product promotions and tickets for seats

15,000 children perish in the world every day
Yet for a game or movie, nothing gets in the way.

So where are our values? Are we so cursed
That our sense for worth is strangely reversed?

The answer is glaring—what dominates our lives?
Whatever we often support, thrives.

Don Aslett

Life At A Slumber

My life so far has been a slumber
Barely rate a social security number
Am I content to just be a nodder
A waste of T-shirts and shower water?

Only dreaming of being a hero
Satisfied to end up a zero
Creeping along, half sedate
Chasing pleasure and fighting weight

Eating, sleeping, ingesting pills
Ambition only for TV thrills
Nothing accomplished to report
A social claimant of life support

Creating no substance to adore
Even family finds me a bore
Then for me when my life is spent
I'll turn to help of government

* * * * * *

If your fit is any of these verses
Stop such self-inflicted curses
Dream of more than getting by
Leave your lazy alibi!

Late Lament

How unkind this verse may be
To those thinking others' time is free.

The surest way to exasperate
Is that careless act of being "late."

Shows ill manners to the extreme
For selfishness it reigns supreme.

Hold up meals, meetings, and projects due
Such nerve—making others wait for you!

It disrupts, disturbs, distracts, delays
One's bad timing makes others pay.

Shows no respect for schedules made
The damage done cannot be weighed.

To rob a bank or another's time
In my mind they are an equal crime.

Don Aslett

Ode To Seat-savers

In every auditorium, stadium, or assembly hall
Is that bad-mannered enemy, brimming with gall,
This self-appointed savior of those who can't tell time
Cheats honest, punctual folks—friends of yours and mine.

Once he reaches the seating, he races to the front
Claiming seats with coats and programs, for his introductory stunt,
Then with kingdom plotted, he guards it from both ends
Reserving seats he claims are his, for "soon arriving" friends.

Spotting seats thought vacant, folks hasten to collect their prize
But find a nervy squatter's claim protecting un-punctual guys,
Even when the hall is packed, only standing room in the rear
A crippled person near age 90, is told, "*Keep these seats clear!*"

Eventually all those mystery guests show their faces at last
Interrupting performers and the audience they've harassed,
As seat-saver jumps to his feet, waving a large overcoat
The straggler tromps over patrons, like a drunken mountain goat.

When those seat savers reach heaven's streets with gold paved
Old St. Pete should simply say, "I'm sorry, these seats are saved."

MANNERS

Hands To Yourself (PDA)

To you caressers I deeply appeal
Let me enjoy the sermon or meal,
Without the scene of rubbing necks
Or giving hugs and slobbery pecks.

When seated someplace I'm often stuck
Watching unbridled affection run amuck,
Out of place especially in church pews
Where furtively they explore and abuse.

Be it a partner or a lover
Intimate times should be undercover,
Don't scratch and paw your seated mate
At restaurant, church, or public date.

To you back-rubbers this applies
For your public chiropractic exercise,
Or fiddling with someone else's hair
Exploring necks and arms where bare,

Out of place is any body massage
Save it for back seat of your Dodge,
Please let us enjoy the public event
Without distraction of hormones spent.

Spare the rest of us, I ask you, please!
There are better places for intimacies,
Restrain from all this shameless stuff
Holding hands is bold enough.

Don Aslett

MANNERS

Rhymes to the Rescue

Dude! That's Rude!

Ungracious as this verse may sound
Some are horse's butts to have around
Insensitive to the world they abide
To be a thorn in someone's side.

They live to cause others stress
Leaving you to police their mess
Their coats and hats never find a rack
What they use they don't put back.

They leave their projects in the way
And their equipment when they play.
Break something?   They don't care
They leave a trail of needs-repair.

They mess up schedules, forever late
Snack left around on dirty plate,
They leave open drawers, unplaced lids
Ignore the plight of free-range kids.

They let their pets all misbehave
Eat the leftovers that you save,
Always look through other's mail
And leave a messy clutter trail.

Continue to nag after hearing,"No."
Blank stupor when it's time to go,
Broadcast their woes, wrongs, and rights
Detail bedroom scenes and family fights.

Every room they use, the lights left on
Shed clothing stays when they're gone,
Your house rules never made the grade,
Their beds consistently never made.

I Love kids and neighbor, yes indeed,
But such bad manners make me bleed,
Sad for anyone stuck in that rut
Of being a royal horse's butt!

Millennial Moochers

Are you living at someone else's expense
On the "taking side" of the charity fence,
Permanently parked in the freeloader's port,
Umbilically-fed with parental support?

A lifetime ticket on the gravy train
Forever pestering your source of gain,
Letting others climb, so you can coast,
An empty hand in the pouch of your host.

Mooching may be an acceptable art
But degree in sponging, not so smart,
Entitlement is thus newly defined,
"*What others earn is also mine.*"

From jobs and school the idlers shirk
Choosing to play while others work,
Content to let others pay your way,
Underwriting your expenses every day.

If you are amongst this sorry lot
Content to live on what others got,
Plan your departure to maintain pride
Give up this parasitic joyride.

If you're not in school or detest a job
Living with parents is a cheap way to rob.
Become a giver, not the one on the dole
Providing for others will enlarge the soul.

Fly the coop, venture out on your own,
Every millennial needs their own home;
Launch with an independence plan
The most dignified course, since time began.

Don Aslett

Hi There, Friend!

A surprise encounter on the street
A past acquaintance that you meet,
Grabs your hand with greatest glee
And babbles out, "Remember me?"

Memory shifts to a blank condition
There is absolutely zero recognition,
That panicked search for identity—
I don't know them, but they know me.

What was their hair color way back then
And was it thirty years, or maybe ten?
A name won't pop to match the face
Can't recall any time or place.

On the phone at least a choice,
"Hey pal, didn't recognize your voice."
You stutter, stumble, hint, and hope
But this mystery stranger yields no rope.

Try to fake it, fish for a clue—
Common friends that we both knew?
Alas, however, time has changed
With body proportions having rearranged.

That desperate struggle for some recall
As they have you against the wall,
You have no wingman to save the day
Deeper in the hole, anything you say.

With no escape, I deem it wise
To just give up and apologize.
Then might come a worse fate by far—
Have a name, still don't know who they are!

To ease your conscience, manners suspended
Too dumb to reveal is too dumb to be offended,
And so the lesson from this verse
Don't ever do the same...in reverse.

Busybody Season

Best leave others' lives alone,
Seems wise enough to tend your own.
Give up the feast of poppycock
Busybodies—in their genes to talk.

Some explore, survey, and spy
A self-granted right to sneak and pry,
No excuse for this destructive quest
It's back-door gossip at its best.

If anything's suspicious in our wake
A surveillance position they seem to take,
A "right" to know what's been "going on"
In others' business where they don't belong.

Serious search for some sensation
Turning interest into an investigation,
Carefully retracing any tracks
Seeking for some hush-hush facts,

Gaining liberties' firm intrusions
Stretching tidbits into conclusions,
Tracking others' affairs, such a waste
That nose should find a better place.

Before they head down "meddle" street,
Must learn the manners called "discreet;"
And not research another's life
But cast aside that carving knife.

Inquisitive hormones are best suppressed
As no one likes to be second-guessed.
If it's any of your business, may it be clear
It's up to the owner to volunteer.

Don Aslett

Spare Us Please!

Your road to recovery we do admire
But of the specifics we quickly tire,
Your personal details we really don't need
Of regrettable habits or some nasty deed.

Calorie count is your private concern
What remains on you or what you burn,
Of the overeating or drinking sprees
Spare us the details, would you please?

Most are realized before you confess
We see the strain on shirt or dress.
Skip the details of how you did it
Allow us space to finally forget it.

When we give our children a loud clear sign
They can sin like we did and turn out fine,
Some waning youth might follow our lead
Indulging themselves in a similar deed.

No need to explain when your good sense arrived
After those wild-oat days you survived,
Your road to recovery we do admire
But of the specifics we quickly tire!

Mother's Day Wish

Many a woman wishes for a Mother's Day
When all televised sports would back away,
So they need not give up deserved first place
To playoffs, tournaments, or any race.

As sweaty athletes take their day
On courts or fields to compete and play,
Men thrive on action live and raw
With commentator repeating what they saw.

Their kids middle names they hardly know
But can validate status of who turns Pro,
Women wonder but seldom say
What kind of men watch other men play?

This male addiction...such a shame
Time, money and emotion for just a game,
Sports help kids develop during play
Juvenile adults strip the value away.

What a glorious Mother's Day it would be
If sports addiction had some therapy!
If we worshipped Deity like a playoff game
On earth would be no sin or blame.

Leagues and playoffs overlap each other
But when is the season just for Mother?
I'm sure many a mother's secret wish
Is to dynamite that satellite dish.

Don Aslett

PLAY

Rhymes to the Rescue

Sacred Ground

Suburbia, when through you I drive
I remember the time when I was five,
Right next door to a vacant lot
We lived! It was our cherished spot.

Rapture from that piece of ground
Echoes nigh a sacred sound—
Smack of marbles, a winner's thrill,
That pile of sand was Bunker's Hill,

Built our forts, nearly four feet tall
With stacking crates, no urban sprawl,
Makeshift capes from flour sacks
To soar around our kid-made shacks.

"Kick the Can," both girls and boys,
No one complained about our noise,
Set up crude bases anywhere
Kites flew high into the air.

"No Dumping" signs were never posted,
No restrictions on weenies roasted,
Absent theaters and shopping mall,
Just hide-and-seek when weeds were tall.

Climb old trees to look out yonder,
Birds to catch and clouds to ponder,
Convert old tire to a makeshift swing,
A broken arm and first bee sting.

Snowball forts, we grouped in teams
For Fox and Geese, with frosty screams.
No need for geography or math
To find our hidden shortcut path.

We rode our bikes over mini-jumps
And got the thrill of new goose bumps,
Secret joy and simple pleasure,
Earth to hide all buried treasure.

The scent of weeds when they burned,
The taste of dust as seasons turned,
When dark our homeward path was clear,
No muggers gave us cause to fear.

Then heartbreak came to us one day
When a new house took our lot away.
We stood in tears, on the sad occasion
And witnessed that concrete invasion.

Yes, holy was our piece of ground
Surpassing even church bell sound,
Indelibly written, the lessons taught,
The life we lived on that vacant lot.

Playground Pity

Apresent dilemma I must confide
I see no children playing outside,
No one shooting hoops on driveway pad,
The kiddies' gym unused, so sad!

Where went dodgeball and Red Rover
The scream and rush from Any-I-Over?
Those rough running races and games of tag,
Well-worn balls and tattered flags

Where kids made up their playground rules
With pretend swords and cardboard tools.
Fewer kids run freely outdoors
Playing hide and seek or tug-of-war.

A mere two generations ago
They played outside in grass or snow
And needed no schedules to jump or run.
Rain or shine, outside was fun!

Squeals of delight are now seldom found,
Seems we've neutered the children's playground.
With great alarm, I have realized
Those little ones now are ORGANIZED!

Never thought I'd see the day
That rulebooks dictate children's play.
Tree houses gave way to modern sports
With well-groomed fields and shiny courts.

Kids are included in some league or club
Signed up to be first string or sub,
Their teams now call for a sponsorship
And other formalities normal kids would skip.

They have uniforms! Insurance too!
There's nothing creative for the kids to do.
They must pick a sport and pay a fee,
Forget about spontaneity!

For freedom's sake, our youth must dream,
Real self-expression requires no team.
We've placed winning and trophies in their way.
Winning? Heck, they just want to play!

Don Aslett

PLAY

Rhymes to the Rescue

The Work Of Play

Don't wish to dampen life's crowning perk
But "having fun" seems a lot of work.

You travel miles to stand in line,
To meet up with people who can't tell time
Hunt for parking...shell out the cash,
Race the crowds, you make a dash!

Armloads of stuff dropped and tromped
Coveting places you haven't romped!
Fighting to translate scribbled maps,
Losing cameras and finding wraps.

Anxiety...and impatient kids...
Spilling goods after losing lids
Intermission, souvenirs...
Frustrated people, some in tears...

Finding hotels, circling laps,
Gawking at lights like a bunch of saps
Crazy schedules and cancellations,
Always hunting for relief stations...!

Struggle for a space on a crowded shore
To roast your body and color it more
Labor with a pack up some sheer cliff
Sleep on rocks till sore and stiff!

Bake in the sand like a side of beef
Then tear up your body on a surfing reef
Drive glassy roads where icicles drip,
Slide down some hill to freeze off a lip.

Dried sandwiches, full of sand,
Rental shops that won't turn a hand
Spending money like a drunken fool,
And eating junk food is always cool!

Losing glasses, keys, and coats
Herded along like a bunch of goats
Locking stuff from any thief
Noise and running, no relief.

And...having fun makes twice the mess
Triple the clothes, would you guess?
And when it's over, there's little there...
Clock and wallet, completely bare.

Don't' wish to dampen life's crowning perk
But "having fun" seems like a lot of work.

No Room For Thee?

Can new love sprout and survive
While old loves are kept alive?

When I get a friend that's new,
Means not that I've forgotten you.

Adding layers does not dilute
Or give anyone else the boot.

New friendships however appealing
Do not cause any loss of feeling.

Love's bonds are not undone
When appears another "favorite son."

Additional members to the cast
Does not doom any from the past.

When I've picked a perfect match
Someone new cannot break the latch.

Don Aslett

The Mean Man

A miserable man moved into our town
Wore on his head a martyr's crown
Had made his mind up far before
That no one would ever defile his door

He built a fence too high to scale
And planted thorns, should it fail
He shouted threats and posted signs
"Beware of dog" and trespass fines

Solicitors dare not breach his gate
His gorgeous home that reeked with hate
He didn't nod at the grocery store
One neighbor's leaves made him sore

For several years he lived this way
And finally packed up and moved away.
How glad we were his stay was brief
His leaving was a great relief!

May we not be of similar fate
If our turn comes to relocate.

RELATI❤SHIPS

Synthetic Life

Caught myself again today
Testing petals in a flower spray,
With closed eyes to get full feel;
Is this plant fake, or is it real?

    The artificial I do fear
    For many are not as they appear
    Technology marvelous, I sure admit
    How man has perfected the counterfeit.

But with all our modern masquerade
What am I getting for what I paid?
Easily I turn over my loot
For an artificial substitute.

    Lab-grown jewelry made of paste,
    Food injected with phony taste.
    Perfume, padding, synthetic milk,
    Rubber trees, and flowers silk,

Digital music, computer art,
Even a manufactured heart,
Remodel our faces, replace our breath,
Tubes in us control life or death.

    Can a relationship be much the same:
    Beautiful, but just a game?
    Things that make us seem so mated
    Will I wake to find are simulated?

Is the love I so carefully tend
Genuine or just pretend?
And those elations that I savor,
Heart deep or surface flavor?

    I wonder about my drive to serve
    Is it love for others or ego's nerve?
    Could it be this thing that I am
    Is scripted imposter, another sham?

Lord, help me in this world of frill
To separate the fake from real.
May my love be genuine,
Authentic and fully mine.

Don Aslett

"With" Works

"With" carries sunlight through the night,
Calms emotions, ends sleepless plight.

"With" validates what's genuine
And ends the division of "yours" and "mine."

"With" settles lonely, wandering minds,
Even in setbacks, adventure finds.

"With" fills in the blanks of "apart,"
Bypasses the brain to go straight to the heart.

"With" quiets wanting's anxious breath,
Can even quell looming fear of death.

"With" heals wounds that absence sires,
And silent allegiance it inspires.

"With" is intimacy, without any dues,
Its presence blesses any quest you choose.

"With" dissolves fragments of misgiving,
Adds rich adornment to routine living.

"With" is that constant deeded ember
Extending warmth, beyond September.

"With" puts an end to selfish care,
Is a sweet amen to a companion's prayer.

Agree To Disagree

When two don't agree—say you and me
Don't deem it monumental,
Opinions made in experience shade
Are meant to be nonjudgmental.

Some sound alarms and take up arms,
Their upper lips get stiffer,
They rant and stew over another's view
Who maybe has cause to differ.

Why throw a fit when you lose a hit,
No need to dig in for war.
Makes no sense to build a fence
Around things we all should ignore.

Contention is spent where people resent
And seldom is the victor a hero,
Outcomes collapse and winners perhaps
Get ratings close to zero.

When we engage in a sudden rage
With passion and conviction,
Forcing our voice on another's choice
Does not give us a strong position.

Different views? We're all free to choose,
Just smile and put tongue on mute,
State your side then let it ride,
Don't start up a thorny dispute.

May not get your way, but you have a say
Expressing your point of view,
Let others vent and watch their descent
Into argument's Waterloo.

Don Aslett

Two To Feud

Arguing and being rude
Poison even the greatest mood.
Remember it takes two to feud!

Why would anyone go the route
Where mature people rave and shout,
And overgrown dummies duke it out?

Because it's always "the other's" fault
We find their wounds and rub in salt,
When we're "sure" we're right, why halt?

A skirmish leads to full-scale war
On truth and logic we slam the door
Forgetting what the battle was for.

In conflict, stupidity always grows
As more out of joint goes our nose,
Or more malicious our verbal blows.

Wounds that open, seldom mend
As other's opinions rarely bend,
Creating perfect climate to offend.

Thus the genesis of many law suits
Beating to death the petty disputes
As best of facts begin to lose roots.

When into accusing, emotions dip,
If we want to preserve a relationship,
Maybe it's wise to take some lip?

Man Picking

A young lass now wiser in choosing her man
Listed the deal-breakers in her romance plan
Those habits she felt forced to live with before
Were the very ones she'd come to deplore.

If he's...

    Had too many jobs or can't keep one now,
    He's growing a belly drinking and how!
    Fully grown, still mooching off his folks,
    Grandparents too he occasionally soaks.

    Sloppy! Never shuts toilet lids,
    No religion, doesn't notice kids,
    He hangs with friends, plenty weird,
    Only exacting in tending his beard,

    Talks about his truck more than his mom,
    Money soon disappears in his palm.
    Little interest in my family's side,
    As for education—he's tried and tried.

    Socially insensitive, a classic slob,
    Asks how much I make in my job.
    He admits to former relationships plenty
    Or is still "finding himself" in his late 20's.

    Loves TV and knows all sports
    Dressed up to him is no holes in his shorts,
    Country music is "all she wrote,"
    Doesn't cook and doesn't vote.

Slacker men, live on your own!
Far better for me to live alone!

Don Aslett

Beauty?

"Cute**"** labels many a lass
"Attractive" others, a share of class
"Pretty" is as pretty does
And truly **"Stunning"** may cause a buzz.

The ultimate beyond these four
Is **"Beautiful,"** which I adore
Yes "Cute" is visual, "Attractive," too
"Pretty" and "Stunning" get looks, true,

But **Beauty** lies beneath the skin
No mascara is required to win.
Beauty borrows no robed pretense
Needs no garnish or jewels to make sense.

Beauty known requires no staging
It's visible beyond any aging
Beauty glows in eyes that smile
Is never, ever out of style.

If missing glamor? Don't despair
Beauty's contest is not what you wear.
Beauty dwells in kindness grace,
Beauty *is felt* in any place.

Independence

Independence is a mode
Where we can so freely run
That in the end we are convinced
We don't need anyone.

We build the dreams that we devise
And exist socially traffic free,
Then our self-reliance
Enables living more selfishly.

Yes, independent people
Choose their own retreat
And learn the self assurance
To stand on their two feet.

But that stand may grow to a standoff
Where love cannot penetrate
Emotions that should be shared
Can become a life stalemate.

Yes, that wall of independence
Built so carefully
Eventually proves a strong stockade
For lonely exclusivity.

Don Aslett

The Summer Holiday

Upon return, the place is still
Lawn now scorched, weeds at will,
Our exit tracks still mark the road
Mice are lodged in our abode.

Leaves gathered near front door
Fallen fruit has become an eyesore
Untrimmed hedge greet scanning eyes
Absence recorded by windowsill flies.

Wind made dust that left its trail
Plants now wilted in a forlorn pail
Peeling paint and sagging fence
Our former living, all past tense.

Tools remain where they last lay
Flowers turned into a weed bouquet
Pasture dry and cobwebs spread
In corners where no one has tread.

Ears of corn cannot be found
Harvest now a burial ground
Time takes a toll when dwellers depart
Defects begin where absence starts.

Beating The Bully

There is always a bully on every block
A Biff or Buster, a jerk or a jock
In all life's venues each kind you'll find,
The muscled brute and white-collar kind.

Oppression is their game, it's clear
To make the "little guys" quake in fear.
They seize upon the conqueror's role
And by position or size take their toll.

Narcissistic, we should mention
By inflicting pain they get attention,
Total mean streak and some hot air
Are two worthless skills the haughty bear.

Use authority they don't really own,
Can't leave other's accomplishments alone.
Weapons, a badge, a tongue, or fist—
Never invited and never missed.

It is pure cruelty, absent love
Finding victims to push or shove.
Pompous goal to intimidate,
Demean, belittle, and depreciate.

So a word of caution for these egotistic beasts
Who minimize others and make them a feast:
In a marriage, at work, or on kid's playground
Don't give them license to hunt and hound.

In front of your face or behind your back
Never succumb to the coward's attack.
Ignore them and you steal their thunder,
They're disarmed if you don't knuckle under.

Don Aslett

Living Saints

In the portraits of life I paint
It's my fortune indeed to have known a saint:
Their time and substance are spread constantly
Truly a master of charity.

Unrequested, unassigned,
Tattered heartstrings they always find.
In their crowded calendar there's room for me
As well as others I never see.

The repairs and rescues that bless my day
They sum up graciously, "'Twas on my way."
Their clock and purse oft bleed for me
Even strangers are treated caringly.

They cushion others' downtime and pain
While their own setbacks still remain.
When the dust of "done" is settled still,
Their hands and hearts engrave, "I will."

They share the burdens that mankind hath,
Have firm footing on perfection's path,
Distributing their portion to those in need,
A share in their affection is a feast indeed.

SERVICE

My Gift

Emerson's essay on my shelf
Says, "Best gift is a portion of thyself."
To exhibit that spirit in charity
Pure gifts must carry no guarantee.

Unencumbered, once bestowed
Never "I gave, so now I'm owed."
Sad is the gift with strings attached
Waiting for a favor to be matched.

True charity carries no refund date
No expiration or rebate wait
Nor is it a bribe on a political plate
Like a sponsorship for a candidate.

Needs no building to bear my name
May I never confuse alms with fame
When donors fail to sign their name
Generosity makes its deepest claim.

Careful in loading the donors scale
Loyalty of needy is not for sale.
The impact of a gift, might never I know
But once it's given—let it go.

Waiting for a kickback for what I gave
Suggests the recipient is now my slave
May my kindness not a marker be
Of any "ownership" of you by me.

SERVICE

Jones' Plot Of Ground

Brother Jones, I met one day, when seeking a helper willing,
Said he, "Too busy to assist, young man; I got to do my tilling;
You see my estate," he gestured wide, "A glorious piece of ground,
No noxious weeds or barren soil—best groomed yard around!"

And that it was! I looked about, not a blade of grass was brown
His landscape was unquestionably the showcase of our town.
I returned to Jones another day, to request his helping hand,
But always he preferred to work on his flawless, gorgeous land.

"I can't bear living on unkempt estate, no matter to me the price,
So any service that I invest, will be in keeping my own place nice."
My years of youth soon passed me by, and each time I went outdoors
Dear Brother Jones just waved a hand while laboring at his chores.

I saw no children or grandchildren ever playing on his velvet lawn,
Nor was there time for any friends, as his hours of toil were long,
Outside his fence it mattered not who pled for help in our city,
Obsessed by soil he continued to toil; for people he had no pity.

Then one hot day as I drove on by, the sprinklers were silent there,
Piled up for sale were various tools, worn out after years of care.
And across the road in a burial lot, I viewed a fresh new mound;
His manicured yard now traded in, for a different plot of ground.

Then later still, I passed that site marked *Final Place of Jones,*
It was apparent by thorns that grew, few cared for his resting bones.
His patch of weeds grew high and thick, briars and thistles sagging down,
Forever marking his burial place—the most unsightly spot in town.

Don Aslett

SERV CE

Ballad Of The Rich Uncle

O'Riley worked at a struggling store
Where life was duty and work a bore,
But he had an old uncle very well heeled,
His fortune O'Riley had all marked and sealed.

Yes, his uncle was aging and used a cane.
As O'Riley inched closer to imminent gain,
He played safe, no new paths he carved,
He skimped and limped and nearly starved.

Content to accept his present condition
Anticipating his coming acquisition,
He never saved or invested a pence
Waiting, waiting for that inheritance.

But for twenty more years his uncle cheated death
Though he had aching hips and was short of breath.
Surviving cancer and a mild stroke,
That old uncle just refused to croak.

While the uncle's life remained on hold
O'Riley himself grew slow and old,
'Til one day gave up the ghost did he,
And his uncle's fortune went to charity.

So... don't lie in wait for that glorious day
When some small fortune might come your way,
The expectation of another's purse
Can easily become a subtle curse.

Careful not to get infected by such a blight,
To another's savings, there are no rights.
If you're looking for someone to gold-pave your street
That person, I doubt, you'll ever meet.

No Rarity Of Charities

I'm willing to reach into my pocket deeper
Accepting *I am my brother's keeper.*
To all good causes? Well, most I guess,
A fair donation...and nothing less.

But charity has its bitter pill
Now hedging into overkill,
There's more freeloaders as of late,
Too many groups passing the plate.

Platoons of do-gooders forming lines
With professionally-made handout signs,
Requesting money to find more answers
For AIDS, diabetes, and all kinds of cancers.

Shriners, Red Cross, Big Brother Foundation,
United Way, Boy Scouts, and Feed the Nation,
Tickets and raffles, and expect a late call
From firefighters or for the Policeman's Ball.

Donate to candidates, clean up a brook,
There's a fund for every cause in the book.
Save gorillas, wolves, endangered snails,
Give scholarships so no kid fails.

Need to sponsor student's dreams,
As well as the games of local teams,
Support school programs or a yearbook ad,
(Junior misses think I'm their sugar-dad.)

The aged and lonely need their helping hand
A fundraiser for the new marching band,
$500 bucks and your name's on a plaque.
Plan to give twice—cause they'll be back.

Now I am willing to bleed for the poor
And listen to the solicitors always at my door;
You'll never see me post a *Keep Out* sign
But can't say how long you may have
      to stand in line!

Don Aslett

SERVICE

The Heal Deal

One morning I was early
At the doctor's waiting room
Observing a parade of patients
With anxiety and gloom.

Diagnosis was mostly visible
On life's well written page
Mortality had made its claim
By accident, illness, age.

A flood of compelling passion
Was quickly mine to feel
If only I had the power
To restore and to heal.

Where is my place to revive or heal
Exactly? I cannot tell
But seems I could lend a hand
In making others well.

The ultimate loss of life—
That I can't control
But the loss of companionship
I have power to console.

There are many professionals
Prescribing the perfect med
I might do just as well
With a loaf of homemade bread.

Any and all who anticipate
A stressful looming fate,
A simple caring caress
 Can readily medicate.

It takes not a miracle
An isolated soul to bless
Because my very presence
Could cure one's loneliness.

I can heal discouragement
And especially neglect
Simply just by showing up
With a dose of sincere respect.

Sure can't restore the blind
But can open long closed eyes,
And obstacles in my brother's way
I could reduce their size.

Raise the dead, replace an ear
I can't go to those extremes
But surely I can raise the faith
Of a tender child's dreams.

As for stress and depression
And their relentless grind
A sincere, lasting friendship
Is the strongest drug you'll find.

Though restoring full health
May not be my gift
I do have unlimited power
To visit, love, and lift.

The skill of nurturing others
Remains a quest to find
Remember true compassion
Lives free and unassigned.

Mr. Lonely

Oh yes, this tale is sad but true
About Mr. Lonely, who will visit you,
When companionships go away
He arrives to torment straightaway.

Alone! And staring at the wall,
Mr. lonely then makes his call,
After departure tears have dried
His invisible presence now at your side.

He eases isolation into despair,
Crowds the mind from hope or prayer,
A shadow fellow, when in need
He'll make your smallest absence bleed.

Waiting? Wanting? Prospects dim?
Self-pity only beckons him,
Unseen, but still he shows his powers
Creating lonely weeks, out of hours.

Though uninvited...he still creeps up
Faith and peace he will disrupt
And defy the soul's best mending kits,
Dumbing down man's will and wits.

Though drink and pleasure might him delay
Mr. Lonely will have his day,
Help from friends, he will disguise
Slightest vacancies he multiplies.

If granted one wish only?
Would cancel visits from Mr. Lonely!
How can one shed this villain pest?
Excuse him—as an unwelcome guest!

Solution simple, don't you see?
Fill emptiness with charity,
When you another's plight relieve
Mr. Lonely then takes his leave.

Don Aslett

SET**BACKS**

What "Ails" You?

Failure has its launching pad
Accelerated when things go bad.

A final plan just didn't work
And all support has gone berserk.

Then when you're sure it can't get worse
Comes extra tax that empties your purse.

You may decide after a full review,
That it's time to try something new—

Never confuse stumble with a fall
Or twenty-five misses as the final call.

Time for encouragement before you quit
Buck up little one! You'll find a fit.

Switch arms when one gets tired
Find an upgrade if you're fired.

Amending, repairing, redoing's no crime
Few great things worked "first time."

Don Aslett

Keep On The Road

When you fall in the dirt and really get hurt
Then stop to sniff and cry,
In sorrow or pain, others stay in their lane
And quickly go whizzing by.

Don't lose your way, at the end of the day
Discomfort doesn't mean stop,
A winner's code is "keep on the road"
Or you'll never get to the top.

Doers don't bawl or let themselves stall
When bad news comes their way,
Sick, or sore head, they jump out of bed
To master any bad day.

To self be alert, because we all hurt
And are wounded to different degrees,
Got to keep moving and always improving
You get little from nursing weak knees.

Be there no urge, must continue to surge
Do it by habit, if you must,
Move down that road in cruise control mode
Or else you'll wither and rust.

People with same view will travel past you
When you stop to nurse an "owie,"
Don't be a wimp when you have cause to limp
Keep progress a constant "wowie!"

Get Over It

I'll not faint, over a few specks of paint,
Or a cuff or collar that's frayed
If a drop of snot, or tiny spot,
Occasionally is made.

A well-wrinkled shirt might hide the dirt
And saves some washday time.
Perfect dress causes closet stress
To keep up with fashion's climb.

So I step in dog poop, or miss a belt loop,
My pants will not fall down.
If the socks I snatch fail to match
I can still face the town.

I'll not be stopped by napkins dropped
My lap will catch it before the floor.
A little sip that leaves milk on the lip
Easily I can ignore.

Miss a meal? No big deal
Would reduce a few "obeses."
So the bread is old, cut off the mold
And eat in smaller pieces.

Residue lingers when I lick my fingers
And the best-combed hair gets mussed.
A little smeared ink on a hand, I think,
Is a creative mark you can trust.

Not spelled right? Don't get uptight
As long as it is recognized;
Some extra T's or missing E's
Punish only a perfectionist's eyes.

Don't get hung up on a cracked cup
Or a tiny fender dent.
Don't report a tie too short
Or to whom an old plate was lent.

Out of step is not always inept,
Nor owning a beat-up watch,
Actions make dust, well-used will rust,
And sweat-stained isn't a botch.

If you learn to abolish too much polish
And settle for good timing and taste,
Accept some terror from an occasional error
The results can override the waste.

Progress can't halt for a possible fault
Or always wait for the "ideal,"
If makeshift will suffice, don't even think twice,
No need to make life an ordeal.

Don Aslett

Project Pains

Contemplating a project that's been on hold
The *I'll do it* promise getting old,
Time to knock this out in a flash
Finally got some time and cash.

Plans and tools now all in place
Plenty of nerve, so clear some space!
Once this project is on its way
It'll be finished in less than a day.

Did similar project just five years ago
Harder now—I'm three times as slow,
Glitches now to test my wits,
Losing parts and nothing fits.

Now every time I hit a snag
The more I sweat and less I brag,
Even my pledge of "never shirk"
Is losing strength when it doesn't work.

It sure appeared an easy task
Need some help? Will never ask!
Confidence then begins to wilt
As I doubt this thing can be built!

Time and money I am blowing
Friends start asking, "*How's it going*?"
All patience gone, nerves now raw
Where is my mechanical son-in-law?

Instead of doubting, just play it smart
Head down the street to nearest Wal-Mart!
Yes, in this pickle we all have been
Time heals memory, we'll do it again!

Reverses

Setbacks! **Will a good man buckle?**
As any ambition will skin a knuckle
Crops will fail, the water will rise
The best Herefords sometimes die.

Rich get richer; poor get poorer
Strained muscles will get sorer
Surest wins are sometimes lost
Harvest often not worth the cost.

Strongest bonds are known to fail
All crooks aren't caught and sent to jail
Ailments come which have no cure
Many guarantees are premature.

Smoothest road will have some mire
A fireproof building can catch fire
Champions don't win every bout
The richest mine will bottom out.

Best performers can do a flop
Longest tradition comes to a stop
So...cheer up man and take your lickin'
You're still alive and still a-kickin'!

Don Aslett

Those Extra Errors

You awake into life's pulsing race
And determine that you're way off base
Realizing you have missed the boat
And consequence has you by the throat.

Seemed a good idea at the time
But all results failed to shine
With no warning of hurt or sin
Logic whispered, "Jump right in!"

Maybe bought something claimed to be true
It bottom-lined a real boo-boo
Perhaps your hormones made the call
Causing plans to take a fall.

Or a careless remark in a passing flirt
That turned intended fun into a hurt
Then gossip with its eager lip
Quickly enlarged what you let slip.

Don't quit the game if you drop the ball
Or be turned away by error's call
The holiest intention can be mislead
A setback no reason to lose your head.

The best will botch a job or two
As all endeavors don't prove true
From childish errors to mature mistakes
A course correction it daily takes.

Please no moaning about bad luck
If you're still breathing, you aint stuck!
Homerun hero was once the strikeout king
Past loss forgotten in the praise we sing.

As for setbacks, you'll get your share
There's plenty ahead, so don't despair
Face the terms, some brilliant tricks
What you fouled up, just go fix!

Making Do

Making do when plans fall through
Or when you've met your waterloo,
Up the creek with no canoe,
And your income tax is overdue?
It does no good to sit and stew
'Tis time, my friend, to just make do.

You can jerry rig or use super glue
Find used parts and switcheroo.
If it doesn't fit though brand new,
Or your best friend just said adieu,
And gossip about you is untrue,
Reverses can't get the best of you.

It's not your fault, but they will sue,
No luck comes from your old horseshoe?
Arrived too late and missed your cue,
Baby screaming for Similac brew?
All your patience you just outgrew,
Adapt, invent, and see it through.

You won't always win what you pursue
But to be a winner you must make do.

Walking When Wounded

Those bodily setbacks...we get our turn
From a hangnail to a crash and burn
Putting on hold our will to win
Until we get feeling good again.

Some discomfort is a part of life
Very few of us will escape the knife.
With wear and age we reach the day
Where aches and pains are here to stay.

Bad digestion, nerves aflame,
Can't even pronounce the sickness name?
Dog-biscuit-size pill to take
That might overcome that old backache.

When those below-par days do attack,
Do we let them lick us, or do we fight back?
However unkind our bodies become,
There's much we can do to overcome.

You may limp, but brother you're moving
And muscles need stretched to be improving.
One can still see with failing eyes,
Can read, write, and think partly paralyzed.

If pushing your prescriptions around in a cart
There's still hope they can repair your old heart.
When ending up in long-term care
Can always drag race in your new wheelchair!

Compared to the alternatives, most ills are tiny
So buck up, man, get off your hiney!
With more kinds of illness than there's time to suffer,
When physically down get mentally tougher.

Before you OD on an arsenal of pills
And waste valuable emotions on medical bills
Transfer the pain from that worn-out hip
And save all the "stiff" for the upper lip.

Detour Or Dead End?

Some advice to every traveling friend
Don't confuse *Detour* with *Dead End*.

In the changes of direction that life assigns
We will often run into both of these signs.

When getting where you want to go
One means "Delay," the other "No."

As most detours include delays
A little patience always pays.

So take life's roadwork all in stride
Explore some options you haven't tried.

It's wise to retrace steps or go around
And course correct to friendlier ground.

If dead-ends cause you to brake
Use the moment, a better plan to make.

Disengage blaming, don't cuss and pout,
Find another, smoother route.

Don Aslett

Child's Play

With all the new electronics sold
Included should be a six-year-old

To help the needs of us old goats
Who cannot program a new remote.

Off/On and Volume we understand
The other buttons are no man's land.

We find ourselves hardly able
To find all the stations on the cable

Not to mention a constant wish
To control the programs found on Dish.

To change from "channels" to DVD
Remains a senior's mystery!

Can't figure out delay, replay, record;
We're doing well to plug in the cord!

And for sure we need a kid's advice
On which remote goes to which device.

Don Aslett

Farce Book

If you have nothing to do today
And want to Twitter your time away
And learn every detail just about me,
There is a great resource, I guarantee.

So...lazy down and have a look
At my latest post on Facebook.
First, you'll love ME just a bunch!
Here's the sush I had for lunch,

And 82 pictures of my last four trips,
Unfortunately adding inches on my hips.
This house is where a pop singer lives...
And here are pics of my distant relatives.

Gosh yes...that's ME under the museum gate
Standing next to my bashful blind date
Next week I'll be traveling to Bolivia
 So expect much more of my Facebook trivia;

That's where I found the perfect recipe
For my aging skin remedy
Watch this clip and you'll know how
To stop dog's bark and cat's meow

Why...this blog might be read by the masses
So just look at ME in my stylish sunglasses.
Well...here is my schedule for the rest of the week
So keep your computer warm to take a peek;

Just use up your life following mine.
This post took ten hours of my time,
Described perfectly in full-color spread
Sigh...it's 2:31; I'm going to bed...

Screen Time

Long ago for a performance we would pause
      As real live acting got our applause
Then silent films arrived on the scene
      With Charlie Chaplin, the movie king
Vaudeville soon gave way to the talkies
      Coast to coast and in the Rockies
For many decades what held our attention
      Was that incredible color-TV invention
Approaching the 80's computers arrived
      And screen-time wars again revived.

The internet sensation entered the scene
      Where each kid wants his private screen
Personal desktops with a faster view
      Create a new kind of viewing glue
Seems everyone can now afford the price
      Of laptop or a handheld device
Society is converting from pens and books
      To Kindles, Kobo's and onto Nooks.
If we suddenly lose track of spouse or teen
      We can find them quick, on a two-inch screen.

In every person's pocket is handy
      A smart phone to pull out as fast as candy
There must be unlimited connection and speed
      And with every app there's another we need
Through smartphone technologies highly prized
      We keep our families hypnotized
As these great inventions dictate every action
Life itself becomes a distraction
Then will we finally the Lord start entreating?
      No need, answers found Googling and Tweeting.

Don Aslett

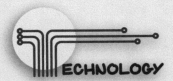

Endless Album

Where once someone took out a wallet,
We now have an electronic whatchamacallit.
"Want to see a picture of my kid
Holding a helpless katydid?"

We hear the words that make us groan,
"I have it right here...on my phone."
Thus begins a family album quest,
Technology at its very best.

So patiently we gawk and lean
Peering at that mini screen.
Lined up like penguins, there we stand
As they search the device held firm in hand.

They wipe and swipe a thousand photos by;
We wait and wait and wonder why.
They apologize, asking for one more minute
To be sure that special picture is in it.

Finally, the shot they proudly show.
What we see? we'll never know.
That portrait found is of such size
Much too tiny to recognize.

Trip Report

How was my trip to Philly PA?
A perfect way to ruin a good day.

I sat by sniffers who snorted and coughed,
Clutter dropped on my head, from the loft.

Four noisy laptops surrounded me,
Two coffee drinkers to slurp, sip, and pee.

Thrashing newspapers, rattling sacks,
Taking up room with overstuffed packs,

Phone conversations just inches away,
Bad weather and delays consumed my day,

Cramped in a space designed for a midget
Surrounded by travelers who squirm and fidget,

Crowding and pushing at every flight gate,
Peanuts and Coke and no dinner plate,

Traffic into town like a parking lot—
No use complaining, the tickets I bought.

Don Aslett

Ode To The Flight Attendant

Into the air that service dorm,
Discipline in trim uniform.
Transporting the dredges of rank and file,
Forbade to "lose it," only smile.

They be magicians, those poor souls,
Pound 20-inch bags into 12-inch holes.
Stretching high, then on their knees,
Bowing to pilots with no personalities.

And surely no human can stay sane
Watching grownups trash a plane.
Up and down to feed, feed, feed,
Too many begging "I need, need, need!"

Passenger mentality one word: "arrive,"
Ignoring all the counsel to keep alive.
Nerds and dorks, all social ranks,
Most not speaking the language of "thanks!"

Taking the flak when the plane breaks down,
Their service perfect, still passengers frown.
How do they do it, day and night,
Handling blame for canceled flight?

Oversold seats or miscalled last name,
Turbulence, they're always to blame,
Deliver food but still hear groans,
People slow to turn off phones.

Help find seating and keep tabs,
Far too many upgrade scabs,
Business coaches, marketing pawns,
M.B.A.s who can't count carry-ons!

The profession glamorous but not the job
Of pleasing the young, the old, and the slob.
Deplane again and open the hatch,
To start over with another batch!

Take Me Home...Quick!

European travel is touted as quaint
But every detail brings complaint
Weather overcast, seldom sunny,
All the hassle of exchanging money.

TV's are tiny, room often dirty,
Flowered wallpaper from 1930
What isn't miniature is old and worn
Room bedding often thin and torn.

Corner taverns with beer and cheers
Sidewalks crowed with souvenirs
No *loo* in sight when you get the urge
Just buying and getting to teatime splurge.

Vacationers in a shopping drift
Compelled to buy some useless gift
Fondling clutter in hypnotic gaze
Shelling out cash like in some daze.

Itinerary packed and nothing's free
What's worth a glance, comes with a fee
Historical sites, even crown jewels!
Look, don't touch, the rule for fools.

Places to step, to stand, and to stare
Reviewing history that happened there
Man can only absorb so much art
Or tend so much luggage in a cart.

We all are wrinkled, over-bagged
Onto customs, we're over-flagged
Surely I've seen every cathedral and dome
Lord, bless the schedule to take me home.

Don Aslett

Ant Antics

It's always the other guy we read about
Who fights the traffic with honk and shout,

Who's crowded for space on subway or train,
Dashing for cover from a Wall Street rain

Who thrashes along in the world of business
With a new briefcase and super ambitious

Practicing and prancing the ethics of callous,
Are we in Salt Lake or is this Dallas?

Measuring meetings, capitalizing pay,
Investing, gaining, every day!

Scurrying on board with line-breaking tricks,
Tromping old ladies with street politics,

Un-chewed lunches, a deadline and rush,
Avoiding the label of being a lush,

A hotel expert with tailored pants...
Gadfreys man! Am I one of those ants?

WE LTH

The Case For Dying Penniless

Dying penniless, a poverty curse?
My perspective is quite the reverse.
Think a minute, how clean and neat
To exit life with zero balance sheet!

A pauper's passing leaves no one grieving—
Much better demise than entitled receiving.
Gone the business hassles and family fights,
No lawyer needed—postmortem delight.

A watch and wallet worn out from earning,
With files and piles that just need burning,
Affairs are in order, so simply relax,
No family burden or steep estate tax.

Ignore all partners and kindred scoffers,
The noblest last deed is empty coffers.
Why leave a wad of unearned dough?
Penniless is the kindest way to go!

Don Aslett

Man And His Money

Money has caused many to weep
Over how much to get and how much to keep.
We bargain, lie...even kill to score it
And it's not uncommon to marry for it.

Matters not if our health is poor
We view money as life's reservoir.
We hire experts to manage wealth,
Secondary to our concern for health.

Our quest to multiply does not cease,
Must find a way to get increase.
Exploring every stock and bond
To push "net worth" a bit beyond.

Bankbook crowded...but it's true
More money ventures we'll pursue,
Follow the market...move it around
That illusive best place is never found.

Carefully, cleverly...it accumulates,
As we strain for best interest rates,
Comes then all of the risk and nerve
To build our own Federal Reserve.

"Tis mine, 'tis his" a slave indeed
That relentless search for more than need,
Wise is "sufficient for our needs"
When man's best efforts fault or bleed.

It's good to have a little tucked away
As life will have its rainy day,
But such a curse on man it brings—
How subtly we become money's hirelings.

Greed Of Seed

Dear parent, you might think this bold
But face it, you're getting rather old.
And should not delay passing on your estate
It could be close...that pearly gate.

Not that you are fading fast
But this chance to give may not last!
I wouldn't think of asking for a lift
But there are deductions for an offspring gift.

My birthright claim, it's only fair
Before the probate gets my share.
I'll take excesses where you have no use
Any cash or car, or whatever's loose...

Your new riding mower sits in your garage
So I'll take it and your antique Dodge
You still own building lots, I understand
Want me to take them off your hands?

I'll keep your lawn chairs free of dust
And I noticed your grill starting to rust.
Gosh, look at all those unused tools—
Why should they end up with some fools?

So sorry I haven't returned your gun
I'll just keep it for a future grandson.
As for those investments you have acquired
Will you ever need them now you're retired?

Sure hope age makes you think more genetic
Cause my credit card condition is quite pathetic.
Bequeath me now, I'm deserving poor
Besides, what do you need extra money for?

For soon comes along that ol' rockin' chair
And footing your bills will be Medicare
So now is the time to divvy up your loot,
Cause you sure can't do it in a funeral suit.

Don Aslett

Lilac's Lesson

Childhood recalls the lilac blooms
Mother gathered to display
Capturing nature's offering
It was my favorite bouquet.

Later, with time and effort
I reached what I desired—
My very own lilac bush
Triumphantly acquired.

Fulfilling my dream and expectation
It beautified each spring
Increasing in fragrance and beauty
Though I didn't do a thing.

This morning while whizzing by that bush
Then glancing through rearview mirror
I realized I have made no bouquets
For more than twenty years.

How like that is ownership—
While life heads to an end
Possessions crowd to ornaments of hope
And become just things to tend.

Having It "Maid"

We're up at five, my wife and I,
Quick shower, eat...then say goodbye,
Off to work to afford this place,
Hot tub luxury and winding staircase.

We jump into our luxury cars,
Dressed just like movie stars
Admire our mansion as we drive away
To earn more money for a future day.

Kids still asleep, but the maid shows up
She'll feed and clothe them and tend the pup.
The nanny owns what we left behind
All our "assets" she will mind!

She plays with the children, quotes nursery rhymes,
And while they're napping, she reads the *Times.*
Soft soothes them morn to night,
The sauna gives her and the kids delight.

Big-screen TV shows a favorite flick,
Of the best foods, she has her pick
A nice dip or two in the pool,
And a nap on the designer couch is cool.

Latest technology cushions her labors,
She samples chocolates, chats with neighbors,
Savors our flowers, enjoys all the art,
Hugs the children, while we're apart.

So who's better off, can you tell me?
Our full-time maid, or us pursuing security?
If objectively we add up the score,
She is living the life we are working for!

Don Aslett

A Prejudiced Poem About Cities

Because I was raised on a farm
Going to town had country charm
A "town" had movies and ice-cream stands,
Christmas shopping and park-lawn bands.

But now that I'm older and business bound,
In big cities I am often found.
A visit there is a sinner's fate
A place quite opposite from heaven's gate.

I move each day past graffiti walls,
Through crowds and traffic and garbage hauls,
Generally beside a sludge-filled river,
A dip in which would ruin one's liver.

Stray cats and dogs, thin and lost,
Birds with feathers stained from exhaust,
Spit on sidewalks, and roadside grime,
All kinds of drugs, and ongoing crime,

Tunnels, trams, and factory smog,
They call all that poison, "city fog."
Sure, those "gorgeous" skylines can bring smiles
When my distance from them is twenty miles.

Don Aslett

My Status

Even though I hate whining
I sure do my share,
Moaning how I suffer daily
But no one seems to care.

In the mirror I look and realize
That the status of "poor ol' me"
Is what I earned or caused
Or am allowing it to be.

"No Fair"

Over daily traffic to get "my share"
We hear the whining, "Hey, that aint fair!"
Life's not a balance of perfect plays
You're going to have some short-change days.

With equal pay for equal jobs
Hustlers often gets same as the slobs,
As luck is known to make its call
You might not get your share at all.
Spend your time for fairness keep?
Brother, I wouldn't lose the sleep,
When jury's back, the verdict in
There's human error, lose or win.

An ideal world this is not
Be satisfied with what you've got
Foul ball or fair, don't count it sin,
Get back to the plate and swing again.

Man may never deal justice well
When there are multiple sides to sell.
Take your lumps, some injustice bare,
Or go around whining, "That aint fair!"

Don Aslett

Mob Mentality

Sign-carrying people march firmly in place
Discrediting others to fuel their own case,
"Sign the petition, make a firm pledge,
Stop all this wrong that we fiercely allege!"

Rallies create awareness and buzz
Mobs get passionate—just because.
Orchestration staged for urgent change,
Protestors yelling in heated exchange.

Soon onlookers join the precarious path
Enlist with no thought of the aftermath.
Causes go viral, harsh statements are made,
And activists join the televised blockade.

Motivated by wrongs that need to be righted
In behalf of all others they deem shortsighted,
To be part of said mob, in behalf of a cause
Comes pressure to join and change the laws.

But protesting groups are often not right
When they build up crowds that freely ignite,
Leads to looting, breaking, and things even worse
That cannot be stopped and are hard to reverse.

Stick to the issues, respect legal rights,
Expect an outcome not now in your sights.
History has proven, with much that we damn
A scapegoat can end up the blue ribbon lamb.

Development Dilemma

Amazing the different messages sent
When the town gets a new development,
It's not viewed the same by all
This thing some now call *urban sprawl.*

Merchants start to rub their hands
Expecting money, expanding plans
Opportunity all trades will feel,
Newlyweds sense a new home deal.

Janitors see more dirty toilets
Environmentalists wail, "*You're going to spoil it.*"
Neighboring families say, "T*hat's enough*!"
The golf course loses some of its rough.

School district shouts, "*We're out of room*!"
The chamber lauds impending doom.
Fire department needs another truck,
Realtors can't believe their luck.

Media gains some fresher news,
Local bar will sell more booze,
Construction noise will shatter nerves,
The bigots forecast, "*More foreigners.*"

City fathers have more to figure out,
Postal carriers adjust their route.
While mayor applauds new demographic,
The road department says *woe* to traffic.

The bigger the project and greater the cause
All standby critics will feast on the flaws.
How can this conflict ever work out?
At least now there's plenty to moan about!

Don Aslett

Works Not Words

He stood quiet before the board,
His merits to review
A humble, modest kitchen chef,
Seeking a job to do.

As for his age and abilities
He certainly could qualify,
But still they asked him, "Finally, sir,
Tell us how well you fry?"

He smiled and leaned toward the group,
His words were free of mocking,
"Sir, I have no speech for you,
I let my cooking do the talking."

Don Aslett

Give Me A Hand

Finishing jobs...an old man's plight,
Using every hour of precious daylight,
He was prompt in life to pay his way
But age has taken his edge away.

Many closed doors he exited through,
With, "Nothing available today for you."
Rejected everywhere he sought
Until one interview he finally got.

When asked for references, about ability,
His answer, "What would your value be of me?"
"Many factors we are required to weigh,
So sir, may I see your resume?"

The boss squinted at an unmarked page
"Your work history, sir, rates no wage."
"No resume, true, but my record stands."
He then held out two well-worn hands.

"Before you turn me away or take me in,
Let me tell you where these hands have been.
These palm scars that first made you frown
Are from shrapnel when my plane went down.

"These burns I earned while being brave;
A child's life I managed to save.
And there, where a wedding band used to be,
As a widower, I raised four kids, you see.

"These hands lifted the weary and nursed the sick,
Were fast to engage a shovel or pick.
And this strong grip, I proudly wear
Carried my aged mother everywhere.

"That missing fingernail is painful proof
I smashed it repairing a widow's roof.
Those blisters are fresh—I never stand around,
I got them this morning spading ground.

"They are long past the ability to write a book,
But I've kept every promise to any hand they shook
I may have some numbness from arctic frost,
But I can tie neatly every sailor's knot.

"Can still thread a needle or swing a sledge,
Or for our country's freedom make a pledge."
That was all the old man had to say
And he took his high-mileage hands away.

I don't know if the old man got the job or not
But a lesson of value can hereby be taught:
On judgment day when it's lose or win,
Hands help manifest where a life has been.

Tribute To Workaholics

Lacking time to sniff a rose
Is a calloused worker, some suppose,
Label is worn near diabolic
By those souls we've termed *workaholic*.

People don't work themselves to death;
They die from too much food and meth.
Still, society scoffs at those who toil
And criticize the burning of midnight oil.

Their many burdens forever in sight,
Personal time is put off till night.
Are these doers in suffering immersed?
Or is the final outcome quite the reverse?

Workaholics might miss a tee-time or two
Helping a thousand other lives renew.
But they atone for anothers' lack of drive,
And through their sweat, others thrive.

Sacrifice created our Land of the Free;
It didn't come from the *average* we often see.
Can we change our rather condemning view
Of those *driven people,* we should look up to?

Please ease up on those we knock
Who choose to labor round the clock.
Their extra effort might compensate
For those whose ambition is sedate.

The Janitor's Funeral

To our janitor's funeral, no one came,
Yet we loved his work and knew his name.
300 of us he served so well;
Where were we then, pray tell?

It's been twelve days now that he's been gone,
No one knows how to keep the AC on,
No toilet paper for backsides,
The lights burned out, and plants all died.

The flies and roaches are out to play,
The flag out front wasn't put away.
There's residue from last night's bash
And for sure no place to put our trash.

No towels or soap in their dispensers,
Batteries are dead in the security sensors,
No one removed the coffee spots,
And there's litter all over the parking lots.

The toilets reek within each stall.
A dispenser fell right off the wall.
Something else around here stinks.
Must I use the dirty sinks?

Fingerprints cover the entrance door,
And there's no shine left to any floor.
All those food crumbs still sitting there,
And no one fixed the broken chair.

Yes, all the occupants missed his wake,
But overlooking him was a big mistake
Because here we are, on hands and knees,
Doing his work. Lord, help us please.

The Power Of An Hour

Ever consider the power
That lies in an extra hour?
Then conquer the urge to sleep or stand,
Don't waste the precious time at hand.

Can clean and wax 5000 feet of floor,
Write three letters, maybe more,
Make a call at a sick friend's door,
Dejunk a closet, its order restore.

A small counter can be tiled
A chapter book read to a child
Three simple meals you could cook
Study thirty verses in the Holy Book.

Plant a small garden with some smiles
Walk three and a half or run six miles
Call a friend, or Dad and mother,
Contact your sisters and your brothers.

Adjust a drawer or maybe two,
Text some pictures just from you,
Clean out and stock your favorite purse,
Write twenty lines of poetry verse...

Don Aslett

Meet My Poetry Partners

Sandra Phillips was the first person to give me encouragement and assistance to publish my poetry—editing and submitting it to the *New Yorker*. For six years, she polished grammar and structure, and submitted my poems to our local newspaper. She has also co-authored three books with me, taught seminars and created TV segments for *Home and Garden* channel. After developing oral care products for children, she markets her inventions worldwide. She resides with her husband, Dr. Reed Philips, in southeastern Idaho, and has raised eight children.

Carol Cartaino was the chief editor of *Writer's Digest* books and pioneered and edited my first 25 books. Her review and restructure of all my writing was done with a shrewd eye. She miraculously de-preached, de-moralized and reshaped scribblings into a productive purpose. She and her son now work as free-lance editors from her farm in southern Ohio. She currently has three new books in the works, and cares for 30+ cats—many of them rescue animals.

As the on-site person to edit, organize, categorize and proofread the selections for this volume, Paula has converted hundreds of rough poems into readable copy—deciphering, typing and improving vocabulary and descriptions on more than 500 poems. She enjoys editing, and owns a busy cleaning business on the side.

Idaho State Journal's managing editor, Ian Fennel, freely granted and published a consistent weekly column space for my poems and enabled a wide readership of the rhymes contained in this volume.

Other accomplices in Rhyme:

- My Dietrich, Idaho country grade school teachers
- The senior English students I taught in high school
- Lindi Smedley, who does layout and graphics with precision and a positive attitude
- Cristian Enache, who created the original cover and sprinkled his artistic talent throughout this volume
- Craig Legory - Illustrator who has contributed to many Aslett books over the years.
- The poets Service, Pope, Markham, Whittier, Shakespeare—and all the greats who kept poetry truthful and simple enough for this Idaho janitor to be inspired